THE BOY WHO FAILED SHOW AND TELL

BY JORDAN SONNENBLICK

Scholastic Inc.

Text copyright © 2021 by Jordan Sonnenblick
Illustrations copyright © 2021 by Marta Kissi

This book was originally published in hardcover by Scholastic Press in 2021.

ISBN 978-1-338-64726-6

10 9 8 7 6 5 4 3 2 1   22 23 24 25 26

Printed in the U.S.A. 40
This edition first printing 2022

Book design by Baily Crawford

To Elizabeth Tuff Duffy, the best
fourth-grade teacher in the world,
for understanding that sometimes
the most difficult student is the one
who needs love the most

The luckiest boy in my class is this kid Kenneth. Last March, when we were in third grade, there was a massive fire in his apartment building. He had to jump from his bedroom window *on the seventh floor* onto one of those fire-department trampoline things. He almost died! When he came back to school, he had the best Show and Tell in history. Now he is a *legend*.

I mean, everything he owned got burned up in the fire, and he had to live in a hotel in Brooklyn for half a year or something. But that is a small price to pay, in my opinion. Because what Kenneth got in return was a treasure you can't buy anywhere, for any amount of money: He got to be special. He's The Kid Who Jumped Out Of 830 Howard Avenue And Lived.

Think about that. If his apartment had been a couple of floors lower, he probably would have just walked down the stairs—still a cool story, but not *permanently* cool. If he had missed the trampoline, he would still be famous at school but wouldn't be around to enjoy it. Every time his name got mentioned, the girls might look up to the sky and their lips might tremble a bit. There might even be tears. The boys would look at each other, thump fists on chests, and say, "Kenneth, man. Kenneth." But this is even better, because Kenneth *didn't* miss the trampoline.

Basically, Kenneth hit the jackpot because some idiot in his building left their stove on, and then Kenneth did a good job of falling straight.

I am the opposite of Kenneth. I am a nobody. I am the un-legend. If I jumped out of a burning building, the firemen would probably move the trampoline at the last second because they didn't notice me. I would give anything to stand out in some cool way, but every slightly unique thing about me is slightly *negative*. You want a perfect example? I am the third-shortest kid in my grade. Not the shortest, because that would be memorable, and I might even get a nickname out of it, or the girls might think I'm cute, or whatever. At least the short-est kid in the class has an identity.

I'm the second-smartest kid in the grade and the second-best singer, thanks to William Feranek, who is the smartest kid in the grade, the shortest boy in the grade, *and* the kid with the best voice in the school. He has *three* things. Three!

I might have the worst eyesight in the grade. Oh, and I was born with severely turned-in feet, so I have to wear incredibly dorky orthopedic shoes to straighten out my legs. But it's not like those are titles you can win in your grade. Kid With Worst Eyesight And Most Pathetic Footwear?

Please.

I get in trouble at school a lot, but not in a cool way. Cool kids have what my grandmother would call *an attitude problem*, but I just have a problem. Until last year, the only problem was that I would forget to pay attention. I didn't mean to get in trouble, I swear. One minute, I would be cutting designs into the edges of a folded paper with everybody else in my kindergarten class. The next thing I knew, everybody else would be opening up their papers into perfect snowflakes, but my paper would just fall down onto my desk in tiny shreds. The kindergarten teacher, Mrs. Kowalski, would ask, "What happened, Jordan? You were supposed to be making a snowflake!" I would be like, "Well, I made it snow!"

Or I would be staring out the window and not notice the bell, so my whole class would line up for lunch without me. Once they actually walked out, and I didn't notice until the door closed behind the last kid. Then I kind of freaked out when I realized I was alone in the classroom with the lights out.

Probably the worst was at the Jewish Community Center, where I went for preschool and where I still go for afterschool programs. Once when I was younger, all the kids had to evacuate. There was a multipurpose room that was a theater and a gym. There was a stage at one end, and the rest of the room was a full-sized adult basketball court. Somebody had left the stage lights on, and the curtain caught fire. When the alarm went off, we all lined up and started walking out—but the emergency exit path took us right through the gym. Every other kid was smart enough to know they were supposed to look straight ahead and keep walking until they got out to the street. But somehow I got distracted by the fire, so I leaned against the wall at the edge of the basketball court to watch. A teacher had to come back into the burning building to rescue me.

So I guess I *almost* got to be a kind of Kenneth, but not the good kind.

I have one other problem. This one is kind of new. It is also very terrible, but not in any way that makes me special. Last spring, I was sitting next to my mom in the audience at a play when all of a sudden I couldn't breathe. It felt like a giant was pressing his giant-sized, giant-weight fist down on my chest bones. I poked my mom with my elbow and tried to say something, but no noise came out except for a weird little squeak.

"Shhh!" my mother said. "I'm watching the play!"

I didn't think that was fair. I hadn't even said anything.

Also, I was pretty sure I was about to die.

I elbowed her again, harder. She turned and squinted down at me in the dark. I don't really remember what happened next, or next-to-next, or next-to-next-to-next, but what I *do* remember is sitting in a chair in our kitchen at home. I still couldn't breathe, and my mom and the father of my long-time best friend B.J. were standing in front of me. B.J.'s dad, Dr. Purow, is my pediatrician, and he was holding a huge needle up to the light, flicking his fingernail against the side to get rid of air bubbles.

Then there was a burning in my arm, my heart pounded like a horse was galloping in my chest, and—snap!—I could breathe again.

"Asthma," B.J.'s dad said. "I gave him a pretty good shot of adrenaline. He should be fine until the morning. Then I'll want to see him in my office."

Ever since then, the asthma has kind of taken over my life. I have to carry around this stupid metal thing called an inhaler and shoot it into my throat whenever I start feeling that tightness in my chest. There are also three different kinds of pills. And allergy shots every week. But first I had to go for five weeks of special testing that was twenty shots at a time—two lines of five on each forearm. My arms looked like they had been attacked by an extremely organized army of ants.

I'm pretty sure nobody has ever become a legend by having asthma. They might have turned kind of blue and made whistle-y noises that made them sound like a dolphin every time they tried to breathe out, but that is not how the Kenneths of the world are made.

Back in second grade, when I would get sad because William Feranek was smarter than me, and better at singing, and the teacher's favorite because he always paid attention, I used to try to make myself feel better by thinking, *Don't worry, you're taller than he is!*

Ever since the asthma thing started, that doesn't really work.

William Feranek might be short, but at least he knows how to breathe.

1. I Am Not Good at First Days

Every year, I get super excited for the first day of school. The week before, my mom takes me for a new haircut, we go to Steven & Jeffrey's Stride-Rite for new shoes, and I get all new school supplies. I especially love new pencils and crayons. I love the slightly burnt engine-oil smell of the pencils, and seeing all the colors in a new pack of crayons makes me wonder about all the new things I am going to learn and draw.

I love drawing. I am kind of terrible at it, but I love it.

Another thing I am terrible at is judging whether I am going to like my teachers. In kindergarten, I thought I would love Mrs. Kowalski. She was fat and had a jolly-sounding, booming voice. I thought kindergarten was going to be like spending the year with a lady version of Santa Claus. I was pretty surprised when it turned out Mrs. Kowalski hated kids who asked questions.

I couldn't help it. I always have a lot of questions. First of all, I wonder about a lot of stuff. Second of all, I miss a lot of directions because of my not-listening problem. Mrs. Kowalski yelled at me all the time. Once, she even taped my mouth shut.

Then, at the end of the year, she tried to tell my mom I should repeat kindergarten instead of moving on to first grade because I had "poor scissor skills." That offends me to this day! I wasn't bad at cutting things up. I was *too good* at cutting things up.

See, I'd thought I was getting Santa, but really I got the Grinch.

I was on my guard when I walked into my first-grade classroom and met Mrs. Gross. She had a gigantic wart on her face, just between her mouth and her right nostril. Her hair was a big, sprayed-up black helmet. And let's face it, the name didn't help. But she turned out to be the nicest teacher in the history of P.S. 35! When I learned to read faster than everybody else in the room (thanks to the fact that William Feranek was in a different class), she let me do projects on my own at a table in the back. It was great. I was the first kid in the class to use a real encyclopedia all by myself, and the stuff she told me to look up was super cool. There were dinosaurs, and baseball stars, and Civil War battleships. I even got to make a poster about the world's first fight between armored fighting ships, the *Merrimack* and the *Monitor,* and explain their battle to the whole class. By the end of the year, I thought Mrs. Gross was the most beautiful woman on earth.

When I headed off to meet Miss Williamsen, my second-grade teacher, I thought things might go well again. The signs were good. She was my big sister Lissa's all-time favorite teacher. Also, she sang to us on the first day. None of my

WITHDRAWN

Search, renew or reserve
www.buckinghamshire.gov.uk/libraries

24 hour renewal line
0303 123 0035

Library enquiries
01296 382415

Buckinghamshire Libraries and Culture
#loveyourlibrary

@BucksLibraries

THE
BOY
WHO
FAILED
SHOW
AND TELL

teachers had ever sung to me. Her voice was beautiful! She sang a song about getting to know us, getting to know *all about us.*

I thought, *This is great! She wants to get to know me! She wants to like me! She hopes I like her!* Boy, was I dumb. Those were just the words of the song, and she hadn't written them. If she had been the writer, the song would have gone,

> *Getting to know you,*
> *Getting to know William Feranek is perfect,*
> *Getting to like him,*
> *Getting to wish Jordan Sonnenblick could be more like*
> *William Feranek.*
> *(Or even nice and quiet like his big sister, Lissa,*
> *Who at least knew how to sit still and follow directions.)*

Second grade was a long year.

Last year, in third grade, I decided in advance that I was just going to hate my teacher, Mrs. Dowd. It probably took me until November to figure out that the reason why she was being nice to me all the time was because she was actually nice.

So this year, I am walking into class with no ideas at all. Lissa had my teacher, Mrs. Fisher, and liked her—but that could be a good thing or a bad thing. I hated my kindergarten teacher, liked my first-grade teacher, hated my second-grade teacher, and liked my third-grade teacher—so the pattern says I am going to hate my fourth-grade teacher. I am not sure that is how these things work, though. When we line up in the lunchroom by the class lists on the walls, I see some good news and some bad news. Two of my best friends are in my class. There's Steven Vitale (The Richest Kid In School, also The Piano Genius), whose mom worked with mine before we were even born, and Robert Falcone (The Coolest Kid In The Grade), who spent a month with me at sleepaway camp this past summer.

But William Feranek is in our line, too. He's smiling, laughing, and saying a friendly hello to everybody around him. He even says hi to me.

That is probably my least-favorite thing about William Feranek. He isn't just the smartest, the shortest, and the best at singing. He's also nice. So then I

have to feel bad for hating his guts, like it's my fault he exists on this planet to ruin my life.

I look to the front of the line, and my heart jumps in my chest. It has already been fluttering all morning, thanks to my asthma medicines, but this feeling is much worse. My sister has somehow never mentioned that Mrs. Fisher is *terrifying*. She is dressed all in black: a lacy black dress with a high collar that looks like it would choke a normal person, plus black stockings and black boots. Her hair is long and black with chalk-white streaks, and it is pulled back into a bun so tightly that her eyebrows are yanked up into points. She looks us over, clears her throat, and says, "Follow me, children," in a low voice that sounds like she has small, sharp pebbles in her throat.

Great! My fourth-grade teacher is the Wicked Witch of the West. What could possibly go wrong?

When we go upstairs to room 4-210, Mrs. Fisher makes us line up in the doorway. Then she gives us our seats. I really don't like the way she talks to us. She sounds like we are already in trouble.

"CHILL-dren!" she says. "I expect that you and your new seatmates are going to CON-centrate and be-HAYVE!"

The desks are set up to make three sides of a rectangle. The fourth side is the front of the classroom, where Mrs. Fisher's desk and the blackboard are. I get a seat to Mrs. Fisher's right. The outside wall of the classroom is behind me, which means that if I lean my chair back, I will be touching the radiators. Above the radiators, the rest of the wall, all the way up to the high ceiling, is made up of tall windows. There is a long wooden pole with a metal hook on the end leaning against the front wall of the room, behind Mrs. Fisher's desk, that is made for raising and lowering the top windows in their tracks. It looks creepy to me, like some kind of weapon from the Middle Ages.

Robert Falcone is one of the last kids to get a seat assignment. There is an empty desk next to me. "Oh, please!" I whisper. "Oh, please. Please!"

I am in luck. Mrs. Fisher puts Robert next to me. He walks across the room with a smile on his face, and everybody watches. This is because Robert has a special coolest-kid walk. I can't explain it, but he looks like he is almost *dancing* across the newly polished wooden floor. Robert has a brand-new 256-pack of Crayola crayons. This is like nothing any of us has ever seen before. Some of us have 8-packs. Some have 16-packs or 32-packs. The luckiest kids who aren't Robert might have the awesome 64-pack with a built-in sharpener. But Robert's coloring equipment is on a different level. His crayons come in a cardboard *briefcase*. With a plastic *handle* on the side.

Robert is like a *professional fourth grader* in a roomful of amateurs.

He sits down next to me with a grin. I smile back and try to slip my 32-pack of crayons into my desk when he looks away.

Once we are all seated, Mrs. Fisher starts giving us a big speech about the Rules for Successful and Mature . . . well, I don't really know what the whole thing is about. As soon as I hear the word *mature*, I give up on listening and check out the room instead. Kenneth, Survivor of Fire, is in one of the seats along the back edge, directly facing the board. He looks cheerful, probably because he is a hero, and also is not dead. Steven Vitale is directly across from me, paying attention. William Feranek, in the front seat practically touching Mrs. Fisher's desk, is sitting with his hands folded, staring at her like there is going to be a test after the speech.

How does he *do* that?

Now that I have checked out the boy situation, I examine the girls. I notice two of them right away. To my right, sitting with her hands neatly folded on her desk, is Britt Stone, The Meanest Girl In The World. In second grade, when we were playing kickball and I tripped over my shoelace running to first base, Britt laughed in my face *while I was still bleeding*. Her secret talent is looking sweet whenever a grown-up is looking, but she is poisonous inside.

My grandfather, who was a science teacher in Brooklyn until he retired and moved to Florida, buys me lots of cool books about nature. My favorite one is called *Venomous Snakes Around the World*. The snake that scares me the most is called the eastern coral snake. It lives in Florida, and it is beautiful. It has bands of bright color along its body that go like this: red-yellow-black-yellow. The terrible thing about the eastern coral snake is that it looks a lot like the Florida kingsnake, except the kingsnake's color pattern is red-black-yellow-black. So you have to remember the patterns to tell them apart. This is a problem because the kingsnake is a good guy that catches and eats rats and other pests, but the coral snake has the deadliest poison of any snake in America. Even its bite is sneaky. It has little tiny teeth instead of big fangs, and when it bites you, you can feel okay for several hours as the poison spreads through you. Then, all of a sudden, the stuff reaches your nervous system and starts to paralyze you. You might not even know anything is wrong until your chest muscles stop working and you can't breathe.

When I look at Britt Stone, I see the eastern coral snake. Beautiful, sneaky, deadly.

Britt isn't as beautiful as Jennifer Deerfield, though. Jennifer is in the front, near William. Here's the crazy thing.

Other kids are terrified of getting glasses or braces, right? I know I was super mad when I had to get glasses in second grade, and I still hate wearing mine, even though I have to because without them I would be crashing into things all day. And when my dentist told my mom and me that I would probably have to get braces by the time I hit sixth grade, that was the worst! Life is hard enough without train-track teeth. But when Jennifer got glasses in third grade, they only made her *prettier*. I bet other girls probably started going home and begging their parents to take them for eye exams after that. And now she has done it again—this time with braces. Every time she smiles, the wires and brackets on her teeth glisten and sparkle across the room at me, like—

"JORR-dan!" Mrs. Fisher growls. "Would you like to tell us the Third Rule for Successful and Mature Fourth Graders?"

Sure, I'd love to. But how am I supposed to know what it is with Jennifer Deerfield glistening and sparkling at me?

Robert Falcone, with his back to Mrs. Fisher, tries to mouth the answer to me, but I am not a good lip reader. I shrug because I don't know what to say or do.

Mrs. Fisher calls on William Feranek, who has helpfully raised his hand.

"Pay attention at all times!" he says confidently.

"VER-ry good, William!" Mrs. Fisher proclaims. Britt Stone smirks at me. I can feel my face turning bright red.

I focus for a moment on the board and see that there are

numbers there for seven Rules for Successful and Mature Fourth Graders. I can't name one, aside from *Pay attention at all times*. Which I have already messed up before snack break on the first day.

I have a feeling it is going to be a long year.

2. HECTOR

Last summer, instead of going to day camp at the Jewish Community Center of Staten Island as usual, I decided to go to sleepaway camp in the Pocono Mountains. When I signed up, I didn't even know where the Pocono Mountains were, but who cared? The camp's owner, Mr. Kiely, came to my house with a bunch of fancy-looking brochures and a movie projector, and as soon as I saw the black-and-white images of Camp Lenape, I was hooked. The camp was on beautiful Fairview Lake! They had tennis! Sailing! Waterskiing! Archery! Riflery! Minibiking! Hydroplaning!

(I didn't even know what minibiking and hydroplaning were. I pictured myself riding around the camp on a miniature bicycle like a circus clown and learning to be a pilot. It turned out that minibikes were just small motorcycles—which was way more amazing than clown bikes. Hydroplaning was basically getting pulled around behind a motorboat on a sort of surfboard—less amazing than flying, but not by much.)

Robert Falcone and one of my best friends from outside of

school, Peter Friedman, came to camp with me for a month, and so did my sister, Lissa. Well, Robert hated camp. Peter hated camp. Lissa hated camp, just because she was bullied by the other girls in her cabin, got sun poisoning, and got pushed off a cliff into the Delaware River by one of the counselors. She's pretty picky about things like that.

As for me, I got sun poisoning *and* food poisoning. I got tonsillitis. I got multiple snake bites. I got into two fights, had an asthma attack, fell off the top of a bunk bed onto the wooden floor of my cabin, learned the hard way that I was allergic to horses, and almost drowned during the quarter-mile swim test when another boy panicked, grabbed my neck, and tried to use me as a flotation device.

It was by far the best four weeks of my life.

At the end, I came home with a new best friend named Hector. Hector is a garter snake. He is the best-looking garter snake I have ever seen. He is mostly black on the top and sides, with a bright yellow stripe down the center of his back. If you hold him up to eye level and look very closely, you can see that just along the bottom edge of his body, where the black part joins the grayish yellow of his belly scales, he has dots of bright red that show every time he inhales. He is also big for a garter snake: nearly two feet long. I caught him during the second week of camp while he was basking in the sun on the shore of the lake, and then kept him in a glass jar filled with grass, moss, and pebbles. Once every few days, I caught some bugs and dropped them into his jar. He seemed to like

the bugs, because they always disappeared overnight after I put them in.

Now that he is home and in a beautiful new twenty-gallon aquarium, he has a new diet. When my mom took me to the pet store for the new tank, the guy there told us Hector would be healthier if we fed him fish. So now on Sundays we go to the store and get a plastic bag full of live goldfish. They are ten for a dollar, which seems like an excellent deal to me. When we get home, I pour all the goldfish and their water into a bowl I borrowed from our cat, Spicy. Then Hector sticks his head and the first few inches of his body over the edge of the bowl, and zooms his mouth around and around until he has gulped down two or three of the fish.

Sometimes I invite Peter Friedman over to watch Hector's feeding time, because it is awesome!

The other good thing about Hector is that he is an excellent listener. When I am sad or worried, I know that I can reach down into Hecky's aquarium and he will wrap his body around my forearm, stick his head between my thumb and first finger, and look me right in the eye while I tell him all my troubles.

Hector has excellent eye-contact skills. He never gets impatient, and sometimes he flicks his tongue out very quickly several times to show that he is particularly interested. And of course, he can never tell anybody any of my secrets.

Hector is the only one who knows my most important fantasy. In first grade, I got the most important comic book

I own: *Sons of Origins of Marvel Comics*. That's where I learned how Daredevil, the Man Without Fear, got his powers. When he was just a plain old kid named Matt Murdock, he was walking down the street in New York City and saw an old man stepping into the path of a truck. Anybody else would have been too scared to do anything, or they wouldn't have thought fast enough even if they had wanted to. But Matt Murdock dove headfirst into the path of the truck and pushed the old guy out of the way! The truck stopped short, but it was carrying radioactive fluid. A tank of the stuff flew off the truck and hit Matt's head. He went blind but gained the special radar sense that enables him to move around just as well as anybody else. He can even "see" in the dark!

What this has to do with me is that ever since I read it, I have daydreamed about saving somebody's life so I can be a hero. I have talked this through tons of times with Hector. My perfect injury would be a broken leg, like my mom had when I was little. She got a big, heavy plaster cast that went from the bottom of her foot to the very top of her thigh. It was so heavy that she pretty much had to lie in bed for six weeks. I would love to have that. I'd miss a month and a half of school, and everybody would wait on me like butlers. Plus, I would have a constant stream of visitors who wanted to interview me. I could say things like "It was . . . nothing. As . . . long . . . as the . . . old man is . . . okay!"

Even Lissa would have to admit that I wasn't just some weak little bookworm if I had reporters coming to my bedside all the time.

So I play this game with Hector. "Arm or leg?" I ask him. "Breaking my arm would probably hurt less. But I wouldn't miss school and I wouldn't get all my meals in bed." Hector flicks his tongue out. I don't know what his answer means exactly. But I'm always glad somebody knows what a hero I am inside.

Especially because I spend a lot of time being afraid. I'm not afraid of breaking a bone or anything like that. My terrible fear isn't even for myself. I am afraid my mom is going to get killed on the New Jersey Turnpike. Or the Outerbridge Crossing, which is a big bridge that connects Staten Island to New Jersey. Every Monday and Wednesday night, when she drives to Rutgers University in New Brunswick, I can't stop thinking about this. I know not one but two different kids whose parent died on the way home from New Jersey at night, so it is not like I am crazy. I lie in bed and sweat over this from nine, when the babysitter turns off my light, until eleven thirty, when I hear her key in the front door lock. I don't tell my mom or dad about this worry. But Hector knows. Hector even knows something worse: Lately, I have been pulling the hairs out of my head while I wait.

If anybody else finds out about that, I won't be a hero. I'll just be some kid who has to see a psychiatrist every week.

And that would be the worst, because my father is a psychiatrist. This has to stay between Hector and me.

By the end of the first week of school, I have tons of new things to share with Hector.

"Can you believe Mrs. Fisher called me *obstreperous*?" I ask him. "First of all, I had to look it up in the dictionary. Second of all, she is wrong. I am not *noisy and difficult to control*. She's just mean and boring. Who wants to pay attention to someone who calls you *CHILL-dren* every three seconds, anyway?"

Hector flicks his tongue out. He understands.

"And it gets worse! She yells at me because she says I can't sit still! But that makes me nervous, and then I *really* can't sit still. Plus, I don't know what she expects me to do with myself when I finish my work early. She yells at me if I read a book under my desk, too. And if I daydream. What am I supposed to do, just sit there and pretend to be a statue?"

Hector doesn't move. He just looks at me from between my fingers, like a very attentive sculpture of a snake. Maybe *he* should be in Mrs. Fisher's class instead of me.

Wait—that gives me a brilliant idea! I will ask Mrs. Fisher if I can bring Hector in for Show and Tell. I will tell her it is scientific. She hasn't done any science lessons with us so far, but there is a long, high table at the back of the classroom with all kinds of old projects on it, plus lots of nature-related stuff like dried leaves, collections of pine cones, and even a few rocks that look like they might have fossils inside. Maybe she likes animals. I can mention to her that my Grandpa Sol used to be a biologist. When she hears that, and sees how responsible I am with Hecky, and finds out how much I know about snakes, maybe she will see I'm not just some squirmy troublemaker.

I'm a squirmy troublemaker with a cool pet.

3. Now Hit Something

Ever since I started taking all my asthma medicines last spring, I have had a lot of trouble sitting still. I keep getting in trouble for tapping on things! My mom has decided I should try taking drum lessons, because she says it might help me focus my energy. I don't care about *focusing my energy*—I just think playing drums might make me cool.

I have no idea what a drum lesson is going to be like. I hope it isn't going to be a complete failure like my first and only guitar lesson, because all I got out of that was a bunch of blisters on my fingers and a total hatred of "Mary Had a Little Lamb." All I know is that whenever I see a live band playing at a wedding, a family bar mitzvah, or anywhere, I just want to stand by the drummer and watch everything he does. Drummers seem like gods. They move faster than anybody else in the band. Their hands go so fast that sometimes the drumsticks become nothing but a blur in the air! Drummers are powerful. They have control of the whole band. At the beginning of every song, nobody can do anything until the drummer says, "One! Two! Three! Four!" The coolest drummers don't even say it out loud. They just click their sticks together to give everybody the beat, and then the whole band comes in perfectly together. It's almost like magic. If I were the drummer on a stage, I wouldn't be afraid of anything, not even getting yelled at by Mrs. Fisher, because if anybody tried to yell at me, I would just hit all my drums and cymbals as fast as I could. And then none of the yelling would even reach me.

I went to a wedding in Brooklyn last spring, and the drummer was the coolest person I've ever seen. He had long curly hair, and when he played fast, it flew all over the place. When the stage lights hit him, you could even see drops of sweat flying

off the ends. But the best thing was the first time the band played a slow song. At the beginning, he didn't do the shouting-numbers thing, and he didn't bang his sticks together, either. The whole band turned to look at him, and he frowned a little bit and waved one of his hands slowly through the air for a while like he was conducting an imaginary marching band. After maybe ten seconds, a couple of the other men nodded at him and smiled, so he turned his head in a little half circle to make sure all the musicians were still looking at him, and whispered, "One-two-three-four-one-two . . ."

When the whole group started playing, all the drummer did at first was use his right hand to play one cymbal, very softly, to keep the beat. And that was all he had to do to control everything that was happening on the stage. I could *feel* it. He was controlling the speed of the song and telling every-body that they needed to play quietly, all at the same time. With one hand and one stick! His eyes were closed, and he nodded along in time to the music for a while. Then he opened his eyes, caught me looking at him, reached down and a bit backward with his left hand, picked up a tall glass full of ice and some dark liquid, and winked at me as he took a sip. After a little while, he put the drink back behind him, picked up his other drumstick from where he had laid it across the top of one of his drums, and used both hands to lead the band into the loud part of the song.

He was so *casual* about all of it! Like, *Oh, I'm just relaxing up here, being the boss of all these professional musicians, making the grown-ups get up and dance, and—while I'm at it—grabbing a few refreshing sips of my favorite beverage. No rush, I have at least twenty seconds until the big exciting part of the song.*

I wanted to be casual like that. Because then nothing would bother me.

I spent maybe half the party just standing there and watching. When the band stopped for a break, I wanted to say hi to the drummer, and maybe ask him how he had started playing. But I was too shy. So I just kind of faded away from the edge of the bandstand until I got back to the tables.

Anyway, I don't know how I can learn to be *that guy* from a few lessons. I am only a shrimpy, nervous fourth grader. It seems to me that becoming a drummer isn't just learning a set of skills. Becoming that guy would be more like a *transformation*: caterpillar me would have to somehow turn into . . . not a butterfly, exactly. Something cooler and stronger. Something *heroic*. Like a lion. Or Robert Falcone, but with drumsticks.

That's what I want from drum lessons. To become a legend in just thirty minutes a week.

When I meet my teacher, Mr. Fred Stoll, I'm not so sure this is going to work. Mr. Stoll is a thin man, a bit younger than my parents, with short, neatly cut blond hair and a very soft voice.

"Call me Fred," he tells my mom with a smile as he lets us

into his house down by the ferry terminal. "And this is my wife, Jottie." The wife, a pretty hippie lady with dark frizzy hair and a friendly grin, offers my mother something called "herbal tea."

This man doesn't look like a rocking drummer. He looks like a *dad*. His name is *Fred*. He has a *wife*. Who makes people weird kinds of tea in the middle of the afternoon. How is he supposed to teach me to unleash my *inner cool guy*?

He leads me down a dark, dusty flight of stairs to his basement while Jottie is busy introducing my mother to their three cats.

Seriously, cats? How rocking can *cats* be? He should have boa constrictors, at the very least. Possibly cobras.

At the bottom of the stairs, though, is **the best room I have seen in my life**.

It's like a secret drum lair. There is a blue-sparkle drum set squeezed in on one side, with a record player next to it. Then there is a workbench with drum cases stacked up all over it, and below the bench are lines and lines of record albums— easily the largest collection I have ever seen outside of a music store. The whole room, from wall to wall, is nothing but drums and music.

Maybe Mr. Fred Stoll is like Batman or Superman. People in the upstairs world think of him as a mild-mannered, cat-owning husband. But once you are allowed into his DRUM CAVE, you see the truth behind the disguise.

He sits down at a stool next to the drum set and gestures for me to pass him and sit on the stool that is actually set up directly in front of the drums—the stool a real drummer would sit on to play this set!

When I sit down, I am kind of excited and also kind of terrified. I want so badly to be able to sit right here and make amazing, thunderous noise, but I don't even know how to hold a drumstick. Fortunately, that is the first lesson. Mr. Stoll lays two sticks down on the shallow, wide drum between my legs and says, "Lesson one: Pick those up." I want to ask him *how* I am supposed to pick them up, but I feel like this is some kind of test.

Mr. Stoll is Obi-Wan Kenobi, I am Luke Skywalker, and I am supposed to use the Force to lift the sticks.

I grab a stick in each hand, gripping them tightly like clubs. Mr. Stoll says, "Okay, watch me," and picks up a second pair of sticks that he has placed on his lap. "See how I'm barely squeezing them at all? You just want to put your hand over the stick, palm down, and then gently grasp it. Most of the pressure should be between your thumb and your pointer finger. Some drummers hold their left stick in something called a *traditional* grip, but you want to learn to play the drum set, right?"

I nod.

"Well, if you want to play the most current music, I think that the grip I'm going to show you makes the most sense, then. It's called *matched* grip, and it will make things easier as your hands are moving around the set. Okay?"

I nod again. Clearly, if learning to hold the drumsticks is going to be a whole big challenge, I want to keep it as simple as possible.

"Put the sticks down on the drum one more time. Now pick them up again, gently. You should be able to control the stick with just those two fingers."

This time, I pick up the sticks as though they are made of eggshells. Mr. Stoll smiles, very slightly, and says, "Now hit something."

4. "William Feranek Has Perfect Penmanship!"

It's only the second week of school, and Mrs. Fisher has already noticed that my handwriting is not neat. By *not neat*, I mean it looks like a dying chicken dragged a pencil across the page because it was stapled to his leg.

And that's when I print. You should see my cursive.

It doesn't matter that she's right. What matters is that she compares me to William Feranek in front of the whole class.

"JORR-dan! This spelling paper is sloppy! I will not accept messy work!" I try to tell her that I spelled every word right, but she doesn't care. "Nobody cares," she purrs, "if you've spelled the words right if nobody can *read* them. Perhaps you should try to be more like William. William Feranek has perfect penmanship!"

Whoopee. I'm sure William Feranek will have a very successful future as a penman when he grows up. But what Mrs. Fisher doesn't understand is that I am not messy on purpose. First of all, my hands are always shaky from my asthma medicines. On top of that, I am just . . . well . . .

messy. When I was in second grade, Miss Williamsen used to send me home with hours and hours of extra handwriting worksheets to do. One night, I traced the letter *e* over and over again, capital and lowercase, until the edge of my pointer finger swelled up in a huge blister.

It was gross. And painful. Plus, my *e*'s still refused to stay straight and on the lines.

The point is, I try really hard to be neat. Just like I try really hard to be quiet and sit still. I don't understand why Mrs. Fisher doesn't just see that I am never going to be William Feranek and give me things I *can* do. I bet I know more about dinosaurs, snakes, and ironclad battleships than he does. If knowing about stuff like that—stuff that is actually cool and interesting—counted, I would be the star. Then Mrs. Fisher would have to ask William, "Why can't you be an expert on reptiles and nineteenth-century explosives like Jordan Sonnenblick?"

Or if she would test us on Marvel Comics, she would see that I know everything there is to know about those. I wish that could be a subject. Our tests could say things like *What lesson does Peter Parker learn in* The Amazing Spider-Man #1? I would answer, *This is a trick question! Peter Parker's first appearance is in* Amazing Fantasy #15, *not* The Amazing Spider-Man #1. *He didn't get his own comic book until 1963—almost a year later. And the lesson is that with great power comes great responsibility.*

I guarantee I know more about Marvel Comics than William Feranek does.

But instead of getting to show people what I know, I am stuck staring out the window of room 4-210 all day, counting squirrels in the tree outside and wishing this woman would just leave me alone. Then she yells at me for not paying attention. Well, if some mean old lady yelled at you all day, would you want to pay attention to her?

But I still try to make her see that I am good for something. On Friday morning, when I am the first one finished with the story we are supposed to be reading in our big, fat reading textbook, I raise my hand and ask to speak to her. I walk up to her desk and tell her all about Hector, and how I would like to bring him in for Show and Tell.

Mrs. Fisher looks horrified. "You want to bring a *snake* into *my* classroom?"

I think I've been pretty clear about this, but I nod.

"Why? *Why* would you want to do such a thing?"

I've already told her. He's my pet. And he's cool! What other reason does she need?

I try again.

"Well, I want to bring him in because snakes are misunderstood. Everybody thinks they're slimy. Or gross. Or dangerous. Lots of snakes get killed every year by people who don't know how helpful they really are. I just want to show the class they should be kind to any snakes they meet."

Mrs. Fisher's eyes get all squinty. "Is it safe for this . . . REP-tile . . . to be in our classroom?"

"Sure, I'll protect him. I can teach everyone how to hold him so he doesn't get hurt or scared."

"I'm sure the *snake* will be fine. I want to know whether the CHILL-dren will be safe."

"Yes," I say. "I promise."

After lunch, Mrs. Fisher tells me I can bring Hector in. I can't believe it. Maybe Mrs. Fisher isn't so bad after all. Maybe when she sees what a responsible pet owner I am, she will decide I am a good boy. Maybe—

"But, JORR-dan," she says, "if that snake causes any commotion, I will hold you PER-sonally responsible."

Maybe this is my dumbest move yet.

The next week, I bring Hector into school in his old jar from camp. I have covered the bottom of it with fresh new grass, plus some pebbles from his cage at home and one bigger rock for climbing. I have also made sure he is nice and full of fish, because I have already noticed he is calmer and sleepier after a big meal. I've even placed a stick in the jar at an angle, so he can climb higher if he gets bored during the day.

As I reach over the radiators to

place the jar on the windowsill behind me, I am pretty sure I've thought of everything.

Everything except Britt Stone.

"What is *that*?" she says in a voice that is even snottier than usual.

"That's Hector, my pet snake. I brought him in for Show and Tell. He's a garter snake, and—"

"A garden snake?" she interrupts.

I *have* to correct her. "No, a garter snake."

"Are you sure that's how you say it? Because I'm pretty sure you're wrong."

"And I'm pretty sure *you're* wrong." I can't believe this girl.

"Oh, yeah? If you're so smart, prove it."

"Fine!" I say. We each have a big, bright red hardcover dictionary in our desks, so I start to look up *garter snake*.

Mrs. Fisher is up front, starting the day with an announcement. "From now on, students who finish their assigned seatwork early should spend the extra time working with this SRA kit."

I have no idea what an SRA kit is, but I am right about garter snakes. The definition from the dictionary says, *any of numerous nonvenomous longitudinally striped viviparous North American and Central American snakes*. I flip back a page to make sure there is nothing called a garden snake. When I see that there isn't, I turn my back on Mrs. Fisher and whisper to Britt, "See, look! It's a garter snake, and there's no such thing as a garden snake."

Meanwhile, Mrs. Fisher is going into a whole long explanation of this kit thing. I catch some of what she says. There are dozens of page-sized cards in the box, and each one has a story on the front, with five questions about the story on the back. Each card has a colored tab on top, and the colored tabs tell you how hard the story is supposed to be to read. The cards at the front of the box are the easiest—pale blue. The ones all the way in the back are the hardest—dark purple. Our job is to start with the first story in the box, and—

Britt hisses at me, "I don't even know what all this *means*!"

"Well, I do," I snap back. This is because I took a class about snakes every Saturday last year at the Staten Island Zoo called Introductory Herpetology with Mr. Robert T. Zappalorti, the boss of the reptile house there. He happens to be a world-famous snake expert, and the Staten Island Zoo's collection of snakes is famous, too. We have the largest collection of rattlesnakes in captivity anywhere!

"It's *easy*," I tell Britt. "Hector is nonvenomous, which means he doesn't have poisonous fangs. *Longitudinally striped* means he has lines that go along his body from his head to his tail. And *viviparous* means baby garter snakes are born alive like people, not in eggs like chickens." I figure this has to shut her up. She clearly doesn't know anything about snakes, and I have a Certificate of Completion from the Office of Mr. Robert T. Zappalorti. It's on my wall at home.

"You're a *freak*," she says. "And I don't care what your stupid snake is called. He's *ugly*!"

I glance at Hector to make sure he isn't getting upset by all this fighting, but he is busy climbing his new stick, so I guess he is fine. But I am so mad, I wish Hector were venomous. Then he could bite Britt, and when she died, maybe Jennifer Deerfield would come sit next to me.

"Hector," I say as calmly as I can, "is an excellent example of everything a *garter* snake should be. Besides, Miss Animal Critic, I don't see you bringing in your pet for Show and Tell. You probably have some yappy little dog that your mother carries around in her gold purse."

"Shows how much you know! *My* pet is a horse."

She's the snottiest girl in the world. *Of course* her pet is a horse.

I give up on the argument and turn back around to face the teacher.

"And *that*," Mrs. Fisher says, closing up the lid of the box, "is how you use the SRA kit!"

I seem to have missed some details.

Curse you, Britt Stone.

I feel even more hyper than usual all morning. I can't wait to introduce Hecky to the class. He seems to be pretty calm about it, although he has spent an unusual amount of time rubbing his body against the side of his rock for the past couple of hours. When it is finally Show and Tell time, all the members of the class sit in a circle in the middle of the floor. I carefully carry Hecky's jar over and sit holding it in my lap. A few other kids go before me, but the whole time, people keep looking over at Hector, whose presence is clearly the most interesting Show and Tell event since Kenneth's Leap of Fire.

Mrs. Fisher makes me wait until the very end of Show and Tell for my turn. As soon as she calls on me, I tell everybody the story of how I caught Hector at camp. Then I stare right at Britt and say, "By the way, a lot of people think garter snakes are called *garden* snakes. Of course, those people are wrong."

Now it is time for The Event We Have All Been Waiting For:

I am going to take Hecky out of the jar and pass him around!

Before I unscrew the lid, I have to tell the class the rules of safe snake handling. "Always stroke a snake from the front of its body to the back," I inform them. "If you try to go the other way, you push its scales in the wrong direction and catch their edges, and that isn't good for the snake. If you are doing it right, the snake's skin will feel smooth and the snake will like it. But if you go the wrong way, it will feel rough and the snake will get irritated. Also, you should never squeeze a snake or try to grab it anywhere, especially not near its head. If you startle a snake, it can bite you. The most important rule is to be gentle. Garter snakes are small, and you can hurt them if you aren't careful when you handle them." I look around at every student to make sure they have listened to all of this. They are all staring at either me or Hector, so I figure they have.

When I turn the lid of the jar, it makes a skritchy noise and then pops off into my palm. A few kids gasp as I reach down to lift Hector from the stick, and somebody goes "Ewww!" as Hector comes free from the jar and wraps himself around my wrist.

"It's okay," I say. "He's really very friendly. Who wants to hold him?"

Nobody says yes. Not even Robert Falcone, who used to hold him all the time at camp.

I start to feel panicked. "Okay, who wants to pet him?"

Nobody speaks, or raises their hand, or anything.

I don't know what to do, so I stand up and start walking around the circle of kids from the outside, like I am playing a very strange game of Duck, Duck, Goose. When I get to Robert, I reach down with the arm that has Hector wrapped around it and beg with my eyes. If Robert, The Coolest Kid In The Class, pets Hector, I am positive other people will, too.

Robert slowly lifts his arm up and very carefully strokes Hecky with one finger.

Whew! I think.

As I start to move around the circle again, some of the kids pull away from me, but maybe half of the kids touch him. Mrs. Fisher says, "No, thank you, JORR-dan," when I hold Hecky out to her, but she isn't rude about it or anything.

Then, when I am almost back where I started, I get to Britt Stone.

I almost don't want her to touch Hector, because she is mean enough to hurt him on purpose. But she reaches out and runs two fingers along the whole length of his back. This is great! Now I am sure she will change her mind about snakes! Anybody who actually meets Hector realizes what a great pet he—

"Oh, *eww*!" Britt says, smiling. "It's slimy!"

Hector is not slimy. No snake is slimy. Their skin is cool and dry. She is just being mean.

I don't say anything, because half the class has just touched him. Obviously, they know the truth.

Britt goes on. "And hey, what's wrong with his skin? It looks like he's falling apart!"

I hold Hecky up to my face, and she is kind of right. In a few places, his skin has started to separate from his body. Now I understand why he has been rubbing up against his rock! I turn to the rest of the class and say, "Check this out! Hector is shedding his skin. Snakes do this every few months, because their scales can't grow or heal like our skin can. When it's time for a snake to shed its old skin, the whole thing comes off at once. A lot of times, the entire skin stays in one piece, so it looks like a see-through snake."

I expect everybody to think this is as awesome as I do. But Britt ruins everything. She says, extra loudly, "No, his skin is *flaking* off. You are the only kid in the world whose snake has *dandruff*."

A few kids laugh. They are laughing at Hecky. Because of Britt!

"Shut up, you . . . you *idiot!*" I explode.

"JORR-dan!" Mrs. Fisher says sharply. "We do not call our friends idiots!"

She's right. I don't call my friends idiots. I call idiots idiots.

Mrs. Fisher keeps at it. "Now, put your *animal* away. Show and Tell is over!"

"But!" I protest. "I haven't even shown you how he moves! I was going to put him on the floor so he can sidewind across it. You have to see! Snakes have several ways of moving, but on a slippery surface like this floor, they propel themselves by—"

"Enough!" she growls. "Go back to your seats, everyone. Although if you have touched the snake, please stop by the sink on the way back to your desk to *wash your hands.*"

Hector isn't *dirty.* But it's over. My moment of glory has been destroyed. Britt did it all on purpose. And she didn't even get yelled at for being mean to Hector. I turn away from the group as I slip my hand down into Hector's jar so they won't see the tears in my eyes.

I hope Britt Stone's dumb old horse throws her. I hope it throws her several miles away, so she lands in New Jersey and never finds her way back to P.S. 35.

When we are all back in our seats, and Hector is back on the windowsill, Mrs. Fisher says, "Well, *that* was exciting. Now, please take out your spelling books and copy each of this week's words five times into your notebooks. And pay careful attention to your penmanship."

Penmanship! I bring real live *science* in, and she cuts me off so we can work on our *penmanship*. I get up to sharpen a pencil, and on my way back to my desk, I hear Mrs. Fisher say, "Ooh, very good, Mr. Feranek. What a lovely even slant your cursive letters have!"

The third word on this week's list is *inequitable*. That means unfair. I don't know why I even have to copy this word. I can already spell it. I already know what it means. And Britt and Mrs. Fisher have just spent the morning acting it out.

5. The Aquatic Adventures
of Disobedient Boy!

When I was four, I taught myself to swim.

The hard way.

We were at the Jewish Community Center swim club, and I was standing on the steps at the shallow end of the pool, wearing inflatable swimmy tubes on my arms. I remember that I felt pretty cold, probably because I was incredibly skinny when I was little. My mom was on a metal reclining chair in her usual spot at the bottom of the grassy hill, tanning herself. She had been reading a book, but I was pretty sure she had fallen asleep because her sunglasses were off.

My mom never takes her sunglasses off outdoors unless she is going to sleep.

Meanwhile, Lissa was with the big kids at the deep end of the pool playing Sharks and Minnows. I thought Sharks and Minnows was the coolest game in the world. Leon, the pool manager, would choose one kid to be the shark, who would stand at the edge of the deepest part of the pool. The other kids would be the minnows, and they would line up directly across from the shark. When Leon blew his whistle, the shark and the minnows would dive into the water and swim toward each other. It was the shark's job to touch as many minnows as possible before the minnows could cross the water and touch the wall.

Everybody who got tagged by the shark then became a shark, too. The shark's goal was to touch everybody so there would be no more minnows. Every other kid's job was to try to be the last untouched minnow. If you outlasted everybody else, then you would get to be the shark at the beginning of the next round.

I wanted more than anything to play Sharks and Minnows, but you had to be able to swim to do that. There was a swim test and everything! When you passed the test, then your name got written down on Leon's clipboard and you could play. I only knew how to kick my way across the shallow end by holding on to a kickboard or, when I was feeling really strong, to doggy-paddle ten feet or so before turning and grabbing on to the wall like a drowning man. In fact, my mom had ordered me not to leave the shallow-end stairs unless I was using both my kickboard and my swimmies.

If I was going to play Sharks and Minnows, something had to be done.

So on this day, as soon as my mom was asleep, I put what seemed like a foolproof plan into action. First, I popped out the little inflation tube on each of my swimmies with my teeth. Second, I used my right hand to pull the rubber stopper out of my left swimmy, and my left hand to pull the rubber stopper out of my right swimmy. Third—and this part was a bit scary—I pushed myself off from the second-to-bottom step and started doggy-paddling as the swimmies deflated rapidly.

It was a simple plan. Either I would learn to swim or I would drown.

The first few feet of my epic swim-or-die mission went fine, but the more air the swimmies lost, the lower my body sank in the water. As the chlorine-tasting water rose over my chin and splashed into my open mouth, I started to panic. My feet couldn't reach the bottom, and the wall to my left seemed very far away.

Without a kickboard, I didn't know how to turn.

I kicked harder and harder. My head bobbed under the water completely for an instant, and then I remembered something the swim teachers were constantly saying during lessons on Sunday mornings: *Cup your hands and pull the water toward you!* I cupped my hands and reached forward for a big stroke. As I pulled them into my chest, my head popped back up above the surface.

I was swimming!

But not for long. Within another few seconds, the last air left my swimmies, and I realized I was super tired and super freezing. I kind of lunged sideways for the wall, which scraped my left armpit as I threw my hands up over the edge. Then I hung on with all my might.

Suddenly, my mom was there. She grabbed my hands and

pulled me straight up out of the water. Then she planted my feet on the ground and started yelling at me. "Are you okay? What were you doing? I told you to stay on the steps! And look at you—your lips are blue!"

My lips always turned blue when I went swimming. That was usually my mom's clue that it was time to make me get out of the pool and wrap myself in my Superman towel.

"Mom," I said, "I'm okay! *I know how to swim!*"

I thought this was incredibly excellent news, but all it got me was more yelling. Then my mother made me sit on our blanket in the sun for what felt like a million hours while Lissa played round after round of Sharks and Minnows.

Some people don't appreciate the courage of a great explorer.

This summer at camp, I learned to water-ski on the lake. It wasn't easy. Before you were even allowed to try waterskiing, you had to pass the quarter-mile swim test, which involved swimming almost halfway across the lake and back behind a counselor in a rowboat. I knew I was a strong swimmer, but the lake water was cold. In fact, it was so cold that it made the boy next to me freak out. That was why he grabbed my neck and dunked me a couple of times before the counselor could reach over the back of the boat, catch one of his arms, and yank him up and in.

After surviving that, I knew I wasn't going to let myself fail the test, even though the welts where the boy had scratched me with his fingernails burned the whole time.

Anyway, the toughest part wasn't the swim test. The toughest part was figuring out how to get up on skis without getting my arms pulled out of their sockets or being dragged a hundred feet with my face underwater. At my first water-skiing class, a counselor named Louise Boily (who was super nice and had a cool French accent because she was from Quebec) told me all the steps I would have to take.

"Number wan: You put on zis life jacket. You pull all zee straps tight. You zeep zee zeeper.

"Number two: When it is your turn, you throw zee skis into zee water. You zhump from zee dock into zee water. You sweem out past zee girls' float, pooshing zee skis een front of you, and wait for somewan in zee boat to throw you zee rope.

"Number ta-ree: When zee rope is in zee water next to you, you poot on zee skis. You lean back in zee water and bend your knees so zee tips of your skis are steeking straight up. You take zee handle of zee rope, and get it so zee rope goes right between your skis.

"Number four: Zee boat driver weel slowly move zee boat forward until zee rope is pulled straight een front of you. When eet ees pulling you a leetle bit forward, you straighten your arms, bend your knees, lean back, and yell, 'Heet eet.' Zen zee driver weel push forward on zee gas, and zee boat weel zoom forward and pull you up out of zee water. You weel be skiing!"

She asked me whether I understood, and I said yes, even though I didn't know why I was supposed to yell *Heat eat!*

When my turn rolled around, I found out that waterskiing wasn't as easy as Louise seemed to think. The smallest life jacket was big on me, which meant it rose up around my neck and shoulders as soon as I hit the water. That made it hard to stay upright without doggy-paddling, but I couldn't paddle and get my skis on at the same time. Plus, once I did manage to get the skis on, I still had to grab the handle of the rope.

You can't doggy-paddle while your feet are strapped to water skis and you're holding a handle straight out in front of you. Even getting the rope lined up between my knees was tricky, and when the boat pulled the slack out of the line, I accidentally tipped over sideways.

Twice.

On the third try, I succeeded in getting everything lined up at once. Then I couldn't remember what I was supposed to say to make the boat go. "Um, go," I mumbled.

Nothing happened.

I said it a little louder, but the people in the boat didn't hear me.

Finally, the driver shouted, "Do you want us to hit it?"

Ah, *that* was what Louise had been saying!

"Hit it!" I exclaimed. The boat jumped forward, and the pull on the rope was so hard that I flew forward and my feet got yanked out of my skis.

This happened two more times before the counselor in the boat said, "Okay, that's all for today. We'll get you up next time."

I swam back to the dock in defeat as Robert Falcone jumped into the lake.

He got up on the first try.

The next time I went to waterskiing class, Louise got in the water with me. She helped position me so my knees would be bent just the right amount, my arms would be straight, and my ski tips would be up. She even pulled down on the back of my life jacket so I could see a bit better. Then she said, "When I say 'HEET EET!' I want you to hold on super tight to zee rope, oh-kay? Super tight. And don't let go." She whispered it in my ear again: "Don't let go. You are brave and strong. You are not zee kind of boy who lets go of zee rope!"

I liked that. I *was* brave. I *was* strong. And I was *not* zee kind of boy who lets go of zee rope!

So when Louise shouted "HEET EET!" I hung on to that rope like a cowboy riding a bull. I held on as my arms and my whole upper half flew forward over my skis. I held

on as my ski tips went under the water and the skis got ripped off my feet. And then I hung on as the boat pulled me, face-first, through the water at thirty miles per hour. I didn't let go until the boat stopped moving and Louise swam out to where I was floating in the deep part of the lake, maybe a hundred feet away from my starting position.

As she pushed my skis toward me through the water, she said, "You have to let go of zee rope when you *fall*!"

I wanted to cry. I coughed up some water and said, "You told me *not* to let go of zee rope! I mean, *the* rope. I was doing what you told me!"

But then she made up for everything when she looked me in the eyes and said, "Eet is oh-kay. Zees time you are ready. Zees time you will keep your knees bent, your arms straight, and your tips up! And zen zee rope will pop you right up out of zee water!"

I turned halfway around in the water and looked at her. She smiled at me and gave one last downward tug on my life jacket. I looked back toward the float, where Robert Falcone was waiting to start his second successful ski tour around the lake. I took a deep breath.

This time, I was the one who yelled, "Hit it!" After a scary half second when I thought I was going to fly over my tips again, I leaned back with all my might, and POP! I was up! From behind me, I heard a whooping cheer from Louise.

What my life has taught me so far is that sometimes *disobeying* orders can nearly drown you. Other times *obeying* orders can nearly drown you.

But at least I am the kind of boy who doesn't let go of zee rope.

6. October Heat

This year, the Yankees are in the World Series for the third time in a row! I have barely been able to concentrate in school the whole first half of October. On top of that, my asthma is super bad right now, so every morning I have to take Theo-Dur, which is the worst medicine of all. When I am on it, I can't stop shaking all day *and* I can't sleep at night. So I get in trouble at school, and then I have the whole problem with not being able to sleep, especially on nights when my mom has class.

I also have a new distraction. Last week, the heat got turned on in P.S. 35. Because the radiators are right behind my seat, my back is now getting roasted all day. After a few days of this, Robert Falcone and I got an idea. We decided to see what would happen if one of his 256 crayons got put on top of the super-hot radiator. Robert carefully selected a white one, because clearly white crayons are mostly useless. I mean, what are you going to do with a white crayon—draw ghosts on black construction paper? Anyway, Robert peeled the paper wrapping off, and then, when Mrs. Fisher wasn't looking,

I reached back and placed the crayon carefully across the metal-grid top of the radiator.

Britt Stone's eyes got pretty big, but she didn't say anything. I think maybe she has a crush on Robert.

For the rest of the day, the crayon melted down through the grid and into the radiator. It was so cool—just like when the Vision passes through solid objects in my all-time favorite comic book, *The Avengers*!

Since then, we have been melting a new crayon each day. The wax has started to drip out of the bottom of the radiator and onto the floor, but Mrs. Fisher still has no idea. I almost feel guilty for this, but it's Mrs. Fisher's own fault for being boring and mean. Besides, the smell is excellent. Our whole room is starting to smell like my house does after we've lit the candles for Hanukkah.

I stay home sick for a few days at the end of the World Series because I have a really big asthma attack. I have to go get another adrenaline shot and everything! The good news is that I get to stay up late and watch the ends of the games, because my parents know I'm going to be absent the next day anyway.

My sitter when I am absent is Mrs. Engel, the nicest and most interesting old lady in the world. She tells me incredible stories of what Staten Island was like before there were even cars. She remembers when the whole island was basically nothing but a forest, with deer and everything! And she grew up in a big mansion in the middle of the island that had a special little elevator called a dumbwaiter just to send food upstairs to her room from the kitchen. If she wanted something, a servant would put it in the dumbwaiter and send it up to her by pulling on a rope. Her parents never knew it, but her older brothers also used the dumbwaiter to send *her* up and down!

I like to dream about what it would have been like to live back then, with nothing but nature all around me, servants to send me food, and fun adventures awaiting inside the walls of my mansion.

Anyway, just as the World Series ends, Dr. Purow says I am healthy enough to go back to school. On my first day back, I get in my first Real Trouble of the year with Mrs. Fisher. Even though it isn't my fault and I am only doing something she has done a million times herself.

When I first get to the room, Robert, Steven, and everybody else want to know why I have been out for so long. I think they are kind of jealous that I got to watch the ends of all the Yankee games, including the clinching sixth game. I don't tell them that I was actually a bit sad at the end of that one, for two reasons. First of all, now there won't be baseball again for *half a year.* Second of all, my dad is a huge fan of the Dodgers, so when the Yankees finished beating them for the second year in a row, he almost looked like he was going to cry. When he congratulated me, I didn't know what to say.

So that was kind of terrible. I felt guilty. But on the other hand, THE YANKEES WON THE WORLD SERIES

AGAIN! It's kind of weird to be happy and sad at the same time. Kind of like the time I fell off the jungle gym at my fifth birthday party and cried in front of all the guests. I mean, on the one hand, *it really hurt*. On the other hand, then we all went inside for ice cream cake.

Back to my point! Mrs. Fisher! Real Trouble!

The problem is that Mrs. Fisher is always correcting people's grammar. In fact, she even tells us we need to be *on the lookout* for grammar mistakes—like maybe they hide behind the bushes on the playground or something. She is definitely on the lookout. A couple of weeks ago, Anthony DeFazio raised his hand and said, "Can I go to the restroom?" She got kind of a snotty look on her face and said, "*May* I go to the restroom?"

The last time that happened, I whispered to Robert, "Why is she asking him? She's the teacher. I'm pretty sure she can go to the restroom whenever she wants!" Then we got in trouble for laughing.

Today when the dismissal bell rings, I get on the bus line in the hallway. The aide who walks us to the bus, Miss Janet, says, "Can yous straighten out that line?"

Well, I figure the right thing to do is correct her grammar. That's what my family does at home when I make a mistake. And that is *definitely* what Mrs. Fisher does in school. So I raise my hand and say, very politely, "Excuse me, Miss Janet, but you should say *you*, not *yous*."

She puts her hands on her hips and asks, "What?"

I need to explain so that she won't make this error any-more. I try to say it in the fancy way my dad or my great-aunt Ida, who is a middle school English teacher, would. "The plural of *you* isn't *yous*—it's *you*. I thought you would want to know."

Miss Janet might not be the best at grammar, but she is extremely fast on her feet. Before I know it, she has charged from the very front of the line to where I am, near the back, and has her face right in mine. "Are you correcting me?"

Well, duh. *Of course* I am correcting her. But I am starting to realize she doesn't appreciate the grammar tip. All I say is "Umm . . ."

She grabs me by the arm and marches me back to Mrs. Fisher's room at the end of the hallway. Great, now I am going to miss the bus for being helpful. When she explains to Mrs. Fisher what has happened, Miss Janet says I am "snotty" and "obnoxious."

Mrs. Fisher agrees. "JORR-dan, why would you do such a thing to your elder?"

This is one of the worst things about being nine. Let's face it: Pretty much everybody is my elder. Which seems to mean that everyone can do whatever they want to me, but I am not even allowed to fix Miss Janet's speech, even though saying *yous* instead of *you* makes her sound like a gangster.

I say, "Well, you correct us all the time. I thought I was supposed to correct people who make mistakes, too."

Her eyebrows shoot up even higher than usual. They are

practically sticking up over the top of her head like devil horns as she growls, "Adults correct CHILL-dren. CHILL-dren do not correct adults. Do you understand me?"

I understand that she is unfair. I force myself to nod, but only the very tiniest bit. And I stare at her the whole time so she can tell I am mad.

"Now, JORR-dan, you will tell Miss Janet you are sorry."

I turn to Miss Janet, and it's hard to talk without my voice shaking. "I'm sorry I corrected your grammar."

Which is true. I have gotten dragged down the hall in front of everybody, I have gotten yelled at, and I have probably missed the bus, too. I am *extremely* sorry I corrected her grammar.

"Well, the next time, you should show some respect!" Miss Janet says.

While I am waiting in the office for my mother to come pick me up, something hits me. If adults correct CHILL-dren, why didn't any adults correct Miss Janet when she was a kid? Then she wouldn't sound like some guy named Mugsy who wears striped suits and carries a machine gun. Once again, the grown-ups are the problem.

This reminds me of that time with the waterskiing. Mrs. Fisher said to be on the lookout for bad grammar. But then, when I found some, I got in trouble for pointing it out.

Once again, following the rules has almost drowned me.

7. I Play the Dictionary

I am super excited for my second drum lesson. I have the brand-new drumsticks that my mom took me to Febb Music to buy. They are Fibes 5As, with nylon tips. Mr. Stoll said that was what I should get, because 5Bs would be too heavy and 7As would be too light. He didn't say anything about whether the sticks should have nylon tips or wood ones, but Mr. Jimmy Febb Jr., who manages the store, told me that nylon tips would last longer. Then he even let me sit down at the drum set that was set up in the store and try a pair with each kind of tips. "See how they feel," he said. Of course, I had no idea what I was supposed to be feeling for, but playing the drums felt amazing. They were even cooler than Mr. Stoll's set. These were made of something see-through and bright yellow. I felt like a rock star sitting on the throne in front of them.

By the way, that's what the stool a drummer sits on is called: a *drum throne*. I don't know what could possibly be cooler than sitting on a throne every time I play my new instrument. Saxophone players don't have sax thrones. Peter Friedman plays the trumpet, and he just sits on a plain gray metal folding chair to practice. And guitarists have to stand all the time.

Like peasants.

Anyway, I hit all the drums and cymbals with the wooden-tipped sticks first. Mr. Febb Jr. asked me, "How do they feel?"

How do they feel? I don't know what they're supposed to feel like. They feel like chopsticks, only rounder and fatter, but I am smart enough to know that would be the wrong answer, so I just nod and say, "Pretty good." Then I pick up the nylon-tipped sticks and hit everything again. These sticks actually do feel different. When I hit a cymbal, they bounce off it better, and make a sharper PING! sound.

"I'll take a pair of these," I say firmly. From now on, whenever I am discussing the drums with one of my fellow musicians, which I hope will happen a lot, and the topic of sticks comes up, I will be able to nod wisely and say I am a nylon-tip guy. "The Fibes 5A is my preferred stick," I will add. "I find the 7A too flimsy. And the 5B is a bit weighty for my taste."

Now that I have a taste in drumsticks, I am practically ready to tour the world with KISS.

I also leave the store with a brand-new music stand, because Mr. Stoll has told me I need one. And my mom says I can get the other item on his list, a metronome, for Hanukkah if I am really good about practicing every week. I don't even know what a metronome *does* yet, but it looks like a very professional piece of gear. There's a whole row of them on a shelf behind the counter. There are some that look like small radios, some that look like miniature old-fashioned grandfather clocks with pendulums on the front, and even some with digital displays on them, like tiny *computers* or something.

I vow right then and there that I will earn a metronome. Then I will be able to say stuff like "I was just using my metronome the other day, when . . ." And if a non-musician hears, he will be like, "What's a metronome?" I will raise one eyebrow and reply suavely, "A metronome is an important piece of equipment for a drummer. I never go to a gig without my trusty metronome! I keep it right next to my Fibes 5As."

Then the non-musician will be forced to ask, "What are Fibes 5As?"

This whole drummer thing just keeps getting better by the minute . . .

. . . at least until lesson number two gets underway and I realize I don't actually know anything about playing the drums. At the first lesson, after I had learned how to hold a drumstick, Mr. Stoll taught me the names of all the equipment: "This drum in your lap is the snare drum. It's called that because there are special wires called snares underneath that change its sound. This drum with the foot pedal is called the bass drum. The two on top of the bass drum and the one on the floor next to you are called the tom-toms." I have a good memory for that kind of stuff, so I learned everything the first time he went through the set. Then he told me what I was going to learn, like how to read music and how to coordinate my hands and feet so I could play beats on the drum set. My only homework had been to listen to a jazz record he lent me and to "try to pay attention to what the drummer is doing."

But at the second lesson, Mr. Stoll actually starts teaching me how to do things.

Apparently, I do not have a whole lot of natural talent.

He tells me there are like twenty-five things called "the Rudiments." He says that if I master the Rudiments, I will be able to play anything. I ask him how long it will take for me to master them, and he laughs.

"Oh, you'll never master them," he says. "Nobody ever masters them."

Now he sounds like Ben Kenobi from *Star Wars* again. I picture him saying, "Luuuukkkkeee! You must master the Rudiments without mastering the Rudiments! Only then can you defeat the Eeeemmmmmpire."

The first rudiment is called the single stroke roll. He shows me how it goes, and it doesn't look hard. All you do is hit the drum once with your right drumstick, then once with your left, and keep repeating. So basically, your hands are just taking turns.

Guess what.

It's hard.

When Mr. Stoll does it, he starts super slowly, and goes faster and faster until I can't even see the tips of his sticks. I can do it slowly, but as soon as I try to speed up, my sticks bang into each other, or I start hitting the metal rim of the drum instead of the plastic head.

"Practice that this week, okay?" he says. "You'll be surprised at how much better you get with practice."

All right, I think. I can practice. I've already promised my mother I would practice.

"Oh," he adds. "Don't forget to concentrate on hitting the same part of the drumhead each time and keeping the volume steady as you speed up. Your hands are going to want to get louder and louder."

I can barely even make myself move the right hand at the

right time, and now I am supposed to concentrate on two other things while I'm doing it? I don't know about this.

Then Mr. Stoll shows me some more rudiments. There's the double stroke roll, which is just like the single stroke roll, but you hit with each hand twice in a row: right-right-left-left. He tells me I should count while I am doing this by saying "ma-ma-da-da, ma-ma-da-da" out loud. "And keep the volume steady, of course."

Yikes!

Then there's the paradiddle, the ratamacue, the flam, the double paradiddle, the triple paradiddle, and the paradiddle-diddle. By this point, I am halfway sure Mr. Stoll is just making these things up. But he writes them all down on music paper, and then starts to show me the basics of how to read music. Finally, he tells me that my homework is to work on the single stroke roll and the double stroke roll until I can play each one smoothly without breaking the pattern.

My head is swimming. I'm supposed to play each pattern with my hands, say the pattern out loud, and read the pattern from some symbols that look like lollipops on the page—all at once?

This is beginning to look impossible. Coordination has never been my specialty. I mean, I was the last kid in kindergarten to learn how to tie my shoelaces.

Plus, I don't have any drums at home. What am I supposed to practice *on*?

When we go upstairs, Mr. Stoll asks my mother if we have

a hardcover dictionary in the house. He says I should practice by hitting that, at least for the first six months. Then, if I show "dedication and determination," my parents can consider buying me a snare drum. Six months after *that*, I may be ready for a drum set of my own.

Well, this is embarrassing! I'm not a drummer at all. I don't own a throne. I still don't know what a metronome is. And forget about the actual drums.

For the next six months, I am a dictionary-er.

8. The Weirdest Thanksgiving Ever

I try to be extremely good for the next few weeks, until Thanksgiving break. And, aside from the daily crayon sacrifice ritual, I think I do a pretty good job. It is exhausting, but then I get six days off! My parents have bought tickets to Disney World, but before the trip, we have a bunch of my mom's relatives over for Thanksgiving dinner. My two great-aunts, Ida and Sylvia, are there, which is awesome. But Aunt Sylvia has brought her husband, my Uncle Gene, and their grown-up daughter, my Cousin Shira. I love them separately, but when they get together, they never get along. The worst part is that Shira has brought her new boyfriend, Carlos, who isn't Jewish. Apparently, this is a huge problem, because when the relatives arrive, none of them are talking to each other.

I hate it! Usually, my aunts are the two funniest people in the world. Aunt Sylvia is very sarcastic, which I love, and Aunt Ida is the absolute best guest, because she always tells me and my sister inappropriate jokes. But everybody is just sitting there, staring at the turkey like it might come back to life and start singing show tunes. Just when I can't stand another second of the torture, Uncle Gene turns to my mother and says, "That's strange. Carol, why is there a girl's head sticking out of your swing set?"

This is an excellent question. We all look out the big dining room window into my backyard, and a head with a whole lot of long, wavy blond hair is definitely sticking out from next to the top of the ladder that leads to our slide.

"I don't *know* why there is a head sticking out of our swing set," my mom replies. "Look, Harv," she says to my dad. "There's a head sticking out of our swing set."

We all sit there for a moment, wondering how this head came to be sticking out of our swing set. I think the grown-ups must be pretty confused about what to do, because it's not like there's a manual for what to do in a *head-in-the-swing-set emergency.*

Then we hear a scream coming from the backyard. I'm not sure the girl whose head is caught in the swing set is *enjoying* having her head caught in the swing set. Everybody jumps up, and my father opens the side door of our house, which leads out onto our back patio.

Lissa and I go running out into the yard and over to the swing set. We have to walk around to the back to see whose head this is, because her neck is twisted all the way to one side. As soon as she sees us, the girl stops screaming and looks me in the eye.

It's Lauren from up the block!

"Hi, Lauren!" I say.

"Hi," Lauren says. She is a year older than I am and about a head taller when her head isn't stuck in a swing set. She lives with her brother, Mark, and their grandparents in a big house on the corner. Sometimes, Lauren and Mark come down the hill and play with me, but I don't see Mark anywhere. Maybe he is hanging upside down in our shed or something.

"Are you okay?" Lissa asks. Which is kind of a dumb question, because Lauren is stuck out in our backyard with her head trapped in our swing set.

"Um, I can't move," Lauren says. Then she starts to cry.

Uncle Gene is the first adult to make it across the yard. "Can you move your head?" he shouts in Lauren's face. I don't know what is up with all these questions, but obviously she can't move her head. What does he think this is—a new kind of exercise?

As the grown-ups gather around, everybody has a comment. I wish they had talked this much over dinner!

"Oh, look! Her head is pinned between the railings," Aunt Ida remarks. "I don't think she can get out by herself!"

"And her hair is tangled up between the two top rungs," Aunt Sylvia adds.

"I think we are going to need some scissors," my mom says.

All the grown-ups nod. *Scissors*, they seem to say with their bobbing heads. *An excellent suggestion! Scissors!*

My dad goes and gets his shiny, sharp pair of medical scissors. As soon as Lauren sees them, her crying gets louder.

"Oh, please, not my hair!" she moans.

Lissa and I are crouched down and twisted so our faces are lined up with hers across the platform on top of the slide. "Don't worry," I say.

This is also dumb. If you're not going to worry when your head is stuck in a swing set and a bunch of grown-ups are about to come at you with scissors, when *should* you worry?

Cousin Shira, who is very good at things like hairstyling and makeup, does the actual cutting. Then, when Lauren can turn her neck a bit, my mom puts one hand very gently on the back of her neck and the other under her chin.

My mom is excellent in a crisis.

"Lauren, I am just going to turn your head a little bit, okay?" she says.

Lauren whimpers, and my mom takes that as a yes.

Lissa and I hold Lauren's hands, which feels kind of weird. But it seems to calm her down. My mom slowly turns Lauren's face while she guides Lauren's neck, and in another moment, Lauren is free! She stands up straight on the ladder, looks at Shira, and says, "Is all of my hair gone?"

Shira says, "Oh, no, sweetie! I just had to take a little off the ends."

That is a lie. The back of Lauren's head looks like she got attacked by a lawn mower. But all the grown-ups nod along.

If Shira's boyfriend, Carlos, thought we were weird before, I can't imagine what he thinks now as we parade up the block behind Lauren. My parents knock on the door of Lauren's house, and her grandmother answers the door.

"Oh," she says, "it's Lauren! Where have you *been*, dear?"

"I was on the swings down the block," Lauren says. I don't think that really tells the whole story, but whatever.

As Lauren's grandmother thanks us and closes the door, I realize we still have no idea why Lauren's head was in our swing set. Maybe we can ask her in the spring. Once she hears the truth about the back of her hair, I don't think she will go outside again until at least March.

You would think this adventure would be an excellent conversation starter, but everyone clams up again before we even get to our house. By the time the relatives leave, Lissa and I are dying. Aunt Sylvia didn't say one funny thing about the food! Aunt Ida didn't even tell her famous refrigerator joke!

If it hadn't been for Lauren, the holiday would have been ruined completely.

While my mom is doing the dishes, I hear her telling my dad that Aunt Sylvia and Uncle Gene have threatened to *disown* Cousin Shira if she doesn't break up with Carlos. Lissa tells me that getting *disowned* means she will be kicked out of their family!

I can't believe you can get kicked out of your family just for going out with someone who isn't Jewish. I know only one Jewish girl in my whole grade, and that's Jennifer Deerfield, who is much too cool to ever go out with me when we get older. All the other girls are Italian and Catholic. Come to think of it, almost everyone I know is Italian and Catholic.

I am either going to have to get much, much cooler before we hit middle school or become a monk.

And monks aren't even a Jewish thing. I am probably doomed.

That night, when I am trying to fall asleep, I start wondering what else you can get disowned for. What if my parents find out I am obstreperous? Or that I have been pulling the hair out of my head whenever my mom is on her way home from Rutgers? Being obstreperous—or worse, crazy—seems a lot worse than just going out with Denise Silvestri.

Before we leave for the airport the next day, I change the water in Hecky's bowl and spend a few minutes holding him. He seems kind of sluggish, but maybe that is because I fed him extra goldfish this week. We aren't getting back until Monday night, so his next feeding will be a bit late.

The Disney trip is great. The best part is when Lissa and I get our dad to come with us on Space Mountain, our favorite roller coaster in the world. He sits in front of us, and when the multicolored lights of the ride hit him, his face looks completely green! When we pull out of the tunnel and into the station at the end, it turns out that his face actually *is* green. Also, he is rubbing his left forearm, for some reason. I think Dad didn't enjoy Space Mountain as much as Lissa and I did.

Lissa and I get along great on vacations, even though we fight a lot when we're home. We always get our own hotel room attached to the one our parents are in. That way, they can check on us when they want to, but we can do all kinds of interesting stuff without them getting mad constantly. Every night, we run to the ice machine in the hallway and fill up our ice bucket. We never use the ice for anything, but it is super fun running through the hall in our pj's and trying not to spill the cubes everywhere.

We also play the excellent game we invented years ago. It's called Burgermeister, Meisterburger, and it is very simple and very loud. Each of us stands on one of the room's two beds. When we shout "Burgermeister," we both have to jump across the gap between the beds. When we shout "Meisterburger," we jump back to our own beds. The goal is to chant and jump

faster and faster, until eventually someone either goes flying off the far side of a bed or falls short and lands between the beds. Or I start wheezing. Or somebody goes flying AND I start wheezing.

Usually we don't get that far because our parents get sick of the noise and bang on the door that connects the rooms. Then we have to get in bed and just laugh for a few hours until we fall asleep.

But once, at a motel in Williamsburg, Virginia, we made so much noise that the manager called our parents' room to complain. That wasn't so good, because our parents actually came into our room and yelled at us.

Honestly, my mom got so loud, it was a miracle the manager didn't call again.

But this trip goes very smoothly. Our dad even recovers his normal skin color, which is a big plus. Nobody wants to tell their troubles to a green psychiatrist.

As soon as we get home from Newark Airport, I charge upstairs to see Hecky. I can't believe what I see in his cage! He is lying on the gravel next to the water bowl, not moving at all. But there are little six-inch-long skinny things crawling and rolling all over and around him. It looks like he is getting swarmed by a bunch of flexible black-and-yellow pencils.

After a few seconds of extreme confusion, I understand what I am seeing.

"Baby snakes!" I shout. "BABY SNAKES!"

My mom comes clumping up the stairs. "What are you talking about, Jordan? How could there be baby snakes when there's no girl snake in the cage?"

"I don't know," I reply, "but look!"

She bends down so her face is against the aquarium glass and stares in. "Oh my God," she says. "Baby snakes!"

My sister and father reach my room, and we all look at one another.

"Uh, Jord," Lissa says, "I don't think Hector is a Hector."

What a weekend! First, there's a dramatic swing set rescue. Next, I find out my cousin is going to get disowned. Then we take a trip to Disney. And now I have to change my snake's name to Hectoria.

9. The Great Crayon Bust

On Wednesday, I can't wait to get to school and tell every-body about the baby snakes. Unfortunately, as soon as we enter our classroom, trouble strikes. The school custodian storms in and tells Mrs. Fisher he needs to speak to her RIGHT NOW! At first, I don't think much about this, because I am busy arranging all my things in my desk while whispering to Robert about the Hectoria situation. Then I drop a pencil and have to bend down to get it. That's when I notice the melted crayon puddle is not behind our seats anymore.

My heart beats even faster than usual. "Uh, Robert?" I say.

Just as Robert turns to face me, Mrs. Fisher's voice rings out like a cannon shot. "ROBERT FALCONE AND JORDAN SONNENBLICK! Come. Over. Here!"

Apparently, the custodian cleans the classroom floors over breaks. And apparently, it takes a lot of scraping to get a month's worth of melted crayon off the tiles.

"Boys, how could you have committed such an act of . . . of . . . *vandalism*? And in my classroom! HOW DARE YOU?"

Robert stares straight down at the floor and mumbles, "I'm sorry, Mrs. Fisher. I'm sorry, sir."

I feel sorry that we made the custodian do extra work. I also feel sorry that now I am a vandalism-ist. But I don't say anything because I am afraid that if I try to talk, I will cry. The custodian is a big, strong guy with a massive belly and a thick, bushy mustache. He looks like the kind of man who will think I am a wimp if I cry.

Mrs. Fisher is *not* letting me off the hook. "Well, Jordan, don't you have anything you want to say? It's bad enough that you are a vandal. Are you also too rude to apologize?"

Oh, I'm a *vandal*. I knew *vandalism-ist* sounded kind of wrong.

I swallow several times, then look the custodian right in the eyes. "I'm sorry about the floor, mister. I promise I won't do it again."

"That's right," Mrs. Fisher purrs. "You won't. And you won't be sitting next to Robert anymore, either. Pack up your desk, Mr. Falcone, and move to the empty seat next to Kenneth." She takes us by our upper arms and practically flings us back toward our desks.

As Robert starts taking all his stuff out of his desk, he doesn't even look at me. But Britt Stone does. She is laughing silently, like a hyena with laryngitis.

When Mrs. Fisher is finished talking to the custodian, she gestures toward Robert's new seat, and he starts moving his things. On his last trip across the room, he finally looks at me sadly. *My friend!* his eyes seem to say.

My crayon supply! I think.

"I will be reporting your behavior to your parents, JORR-dan. Just *wait* until parent-teacher conferences," Mrs. Fisher hisses to me at the end of the day.

I would like to wait longer than that.

My parents say I have to "get rid of" the baby snakes. I argue about it for days, but they don't give in. I think they are pretty mad about this whole crayon-melting thing. My dad tells me he is disappointed in me, which is the absolute worst thing he could say. He never curses, he never hits, and he almost never yells, so when he says he is disappointed in one of us, that is like his version of dropping a nuclear bomb.

I have no choice. It looks like either the baby snakes are disowned or *I* am.

There were twenty of them when we got home from Florida, but I have found two of them dead in Hecky's cage in just a week. When one dies, it is the worst. One got completely stiff and straight, so he was even *more* like a pencil. The other got stiff, too, but it curled up really tightly into a tiny pile of coils. Picking that one up to take him outside to the garbage can was horrible, like carrying a sad little Slinky with eyeballs.

When my parents said "get rid of," I am sure they didn't mean "kill."

Pretty sure.

After a lot of begging, my mom says I can keep two of

Hecky's babies. The only chance the remaining sixteen babies have is if I can give them away to good homes. I beg all my friends. Peter Friedman, B.J., Robert, Steven Vitale, and a third grader named Jonah Carp take two each. This still leaves me with six. My mom drives me to the parking lot of the Jewish Community Center swim club with Hecky's aquarium in the trunk. I ask if I can have a moment alone with Hecky to explain things before we do the meanest thing I have ever done, which is to let these defenseless little babies loose into the wild forests of Staten Island.

It's almost winter. Time for hibernating. But the babies haven't had time to get fattened up. I am practically sending them in front of a firing squad.

My mother and Lissa give me looks as I pick Hectoria up and take a few steps away from the car and into the edge of the woods, but I don't care. I am much more upset that I am a homewrecker.

"Hecky," I say, "I am so, so sorry, but we have to let your babies go. I think this forest will be a nice home for them, at least." I walk a bit farther, down away from the edge of the parking lot, where I know there is a small stream. When we get to the widest part of the stream, where it bends, I hold Hecky up so she can get a good look. "See? There are ferns all around here for shade, and the ground is nice and sandy. In the summer, your babies can lie here to bask in the sun. And if they get too hot, they can go in the water or hide out under the ferns. It's nice, right?"

Hecky turns her head and looks me in the eye. She knows I am a liar. This is a stupid little swamp, and her babies are doomed.

I go back to the car, and I am completely crying as I put Hecky in the cage. I take each baby, one at a time, down to the sandy bank of the stream, where I put them down as gently as I can. When I go to take the last baby out, Lissa says, "WAIT! What if I keep that one?"

I hold my breath, or at least I try to. It's kind of difficult because I am sobbing.

My mother says, "Will you be a responsible pet owner?"

This is a fair question. Lissa is a fantastically good hamster parent and kept our first-ever pet, a very fat hamster named Freddy, alive for something like four years. On the other hand, when I was in second grade, she begged and begged my parents to let her pick out a kitten from a litter that an old lady was giving away for free. When they gave in, she chose a beautiful black-and-white one and named him Spicy. Lissa promised she would do everything the cat needed, but in the two years since then, my dad has basically been the only one who takes care of Spicy. He refills Spicy's milk bowl every morning and takes care of opening a new can of cat food for him twice a day.

And our mom has already had to take Spicy to the veterinarian a bunch of times. It's always really expensive, and the whole way home from the vet, she always says, "This is some free cat, Lissa," at least three times.

I don't know what kind of snake owner Lissa will be. That depends on whether a baby snake is more like a hamster or more like a kitten. But at least the baby won't be out in the middle of the woods in winter, freezing into a hard little pencil-shaped Popsicle.

My mom says yes, and I want to hug my sister.

I mean, I *don't* hug my sister. But the thought crosses my mind. Briefly.

We stop by the pet store down Victory Boulevard on the way home and get a nice new aquarium for the baby. Lissa names him Stripe, which I think is kind of dumb. Every single garter snake in the entire universe has the exact same yellow stripe, so why would you call this particular one Stripe?

It would be like a person naming their kid Two Eyes or something.

On the other hand, I think it's better for the baby to have an embarrassing name than to be dead.

A couple of weeks later, my mom has her conference with Mrs. Fisher. I sit down alone on one of the three chairs that are lined up just outside the classroom door. I try not to eavesdrop, mostly because I am pretty positive I don't want to know what Mrs. Fisher is telling my mother about me.

I hear one sentence very clearly, though: "JORR-dan will *never* amount to *anything*!"

A few minutes later, my mom comes stomping out, grasps my upper arm so her fingernails are digging into me, and practically drags me down the hall and out to the car. She looks so mad I am afraid to say anything. In second grade, my parents were super upset when Miss Williamsen wrote *Jordan's listening skills need improvement* on the back of my report card. I mean, for like a week it was clear that my dad was *disappointed in* me.

I figure that "JORR-dan will *never* amount to *anything*!" is way worse than that.

I just hope if they're going to disown me, they wait until after Hanukkah.

Unfortunately, I am not good at staying quiet, especially when I am nervous. I only make it three blocks. When we are waiting to get through the traffic light at the corner of Clove Road and Victory Boulevard, I ask, "Mom, what did Mrs. Fisher say? Are you mad at me?"

She turns to me, and there are tears in her eyes. I am the worst kid ever. *I have made my mother cry.* "Oh, Jord," she says. "Oh, Jord."

10. Magic!

By the time I have taken six or seven lessons, I decide Mr. and Mrs. Stoll are like magic people. I mean, the whole reason why I am here is because drumming is magic to me, and I want Mr. Stoll to teach me how to do it. But they have another kind of magic: They are *serene*.

I first found out what this word means in second grade when Miss Williamsen read us *The Trumpet of the Swan*. The main character is a boy swan named Louis, and he is in love with a girl swan named Serena. Miss Williamsen told us that Serena's name is from the word *serene*, meaning calm, peaceful, and untroubled.

When I am sitting in the Stolls' living room and waiting for a drum lesson, I feel like all my worries are far away. Mrs. Stoll always gives me a cup of tea and some kind of snack she has just finished baking. Then she asks me all kinds of questions about what is going on in my life, and she really *listens* when I answer. The Stolls have a cat named Cee Cee, who doesn't have a tail. At one of my first lessons, Mrs. Stoll saw me looking at where Cee Cee's tail should be, and chuckled. She told me there was nothing wrong with Cee Cee. She was just a special kind of cat called a Manx, and that most Manx cats didn't have tails. She also said that Manxes were mellow and friendly. That makes sense, because a lot of times, Cee Cee comes over to me on the couch and puts her head in my lap.

Cat fur makes me wheeze, because I am completely allergic, but I don't even care because Cee Cee likes me so much. Spicy would never put his head on my lap unless it was a trick to make me relax so he could sink his claws into my leg.

At the Stolls' house, even the *cats* are serene.

Here is the perfect example of Mrs. Stoll's personality. One day in the middle of a conversation, she pulls on a strand of her long, wavy hair so it is straight out in front of her eyes. Most of her hair is jet-black, but the hairs in her hand are almost white. "My hair is getting so gray!" she says. Then she throws back her head and laughs. I have never met a lady who laughs about gray hairs before. My mother dyes her hair black, and if she even finds one gray hair, she gets super annoyed. Once, at Burger King, I asked how long she had been dyeing it, and a lady behind us laughed. My mom pinched my arm really hard, and then she barely talked to me the whole meal.

My grandma and her two sisters are the same way. They go to the hair salon every week to get their hair colored and then they sit under big, round helmet things that heat their heads up and make their hair curly.

But Mrs. Stoll finds her gray hair *amusing*. It's like she is a Manx person.

Mr. Stoll is super mellow, too. When I do well, he smiles serenely and nods. When I mess up, he just says, "Again." He never sounds mad, or frustrated, or *disappointed in you, Jordan*. And the way he is so nice about it just makes me want to do even better.

I have been practicing on my dictionary every night. I am pretty sure I am getting kind of good at my rudiments, because every week I am getting a bit faster with them, and I almost never bang my sticks together or drop one. I am even starting to get the hang of reading music. I can read whole notes, half notes, quarter notes, and even eighth notes! (My mom seems to find it funny when I sit in front of my dictionary and hit it in patterns while counting "One-and-two-and-three-and-four-and" out loud, but I am proud, because I am learning the *secret language of musicians*.)

I feel like I am getting pretty advanced until Mr. Stoll tells me it is time to work on *keeping time*. Now that my wrists and hands kind of know what they are doing, he says it is time to go from just banging on my dictionary to making music. I don't know how this is supposed to work. When real drummers like Mr. Stoll make music, they have all different kinds of drums and cymbals to hit in order to make different noises. What am I supposed to do—set up an encyclopedia and some paperbacks around the dictionary to make a little set?

Mr. Stoll says that keeping time is the essence of being a drummer. He makes me switch seats with him so he is in front of the drum set, and puts an album on the record player behind us. I don't know what the music is at first, but from the opening note, I feel like my life has changed. I can't explain it, but hearing this song makes me feel like I have only been seeing black and white all these years, and now the world has color.

The song is called "Drive My Car." The band is the Beatles.

There is a short guitar introduction. Then Mr. Stoll plays a roll on two of the tom-toms before starting to play an amazing beat. I don't know how he does it all! One hand is on the snare drum, the other is playing a pair of cymbals called the hi-hats, which open and close if you push your left foot down on a pedal, and his right foot is working the pedal that hits the bass drum. Every time the bass drum thumps, it is like a bright blue shock in the center of my chest. There is also a clanking noise on every beat of the song that lights up the inside of my mind in dark red pulses. I have no idea what that sound is, but it makes me feel wild, like I am about to jump up out of my chair and yell.

Sometimes the drums stop for a moment and then start again. Sometimes Mr. Stoll breaks out from the steady beat to do another wild roll around the tom-toms. Sometimes he turns and *talks to me* in the middle of all this. But he never, ever stops being in perfect time with the record.

When the song finishes and Mr. Stoll picks the needle up off the record, I want to clap. I want to cheer. I am overwhelmed.

Mr. Stoll says, "Now I am going to play the song again, but you are going to keep time." He hands me a weird blocky metal thing that looks like one of the bells you might see around a cow's neck in a cartoon, and tells me I am going to hold it in one hand and use my other hand to hit it with a drumstick.

"What is this thing called?" I ask.

"A cowbell," Mr. Stoll replies. Well, that makes sense. "Did you hear the clanking sound on every beat of the song?"

I nod.

"All you have to do is hit the cowbell along with the clanks, and together you and I will be a *percussion section*."

I smile. A percussion section sounds like something a professional musician would be in.

"Ready?" he asks.

I nod, and he puts the needle down onto the beginning of the song again.

"I'll tell you when," he says.

I hold the cowbell in my left hand, and a Fibes 5A stick (with nylon tip!) in the other. The guitar chimes through the speaker, and as Mr. Stoll's hands flash across the tom-toms, he sings out, "Now!"

I try to hit the cowbell in time with the song, but that is much harder than it sounds. I could hear the cowbell on the record perfectly the first time the song played, but as soon as I start making noise, I drown the recorded cowbell out. When my time starts to drift, Mr. Stoll looks over at me and counts out the rhythm: "One! Two! Three! Four!"

This happens a few times, but Mr. Stoll only smiles and keeps counting.

The third time through the record, Mr. Stoll doesn't play. He just watches me and counts. I think I am starting to feel the rhythm on my own. It feels like lightning flashing in my brain.

I *like* it.

We work on my double stroke roll for a while after we are finished with the Beatles, and then comes a moment I know I will remember for the rest of my life. Mr. Stoll carefully takes the album, *Yesterday and Today*, off the player and carefully puts it into its protective paper sleeve, then slides the sleeve inside the cardboard album cover and hands the whole thing to me.

"The Beatles," he says. "So good. John, Paul, George, and Ringo. Ringo is the drummer. You can learn a lot from these guys. Take this for the week, and practice hitting your dictionary in time with the different songs. You have a record player at home, right?"

I nod. Really, *I* don't exactly have a record player, but Lissa does.

"Just promise me you'll take care of the album. You know how to hold it by its edges, right?"

I nod again, very enthusiastically. I will treat this album like a precious jewel. I will treat this album like gold. I will treat this album like I treat Hectoria. I won't even *think* about hurling it across Lissa's room like a Frisbee, the way I threw her *Saturday Night Fever* soundtrack record when she wouldn't stop calling me names that one time.

"Great," he says. "I trust you."

My drum teacher *trusts me*.

I walk out of there feeling so excited I might explode. I am holding "Drive My Car" in my own two hands. And there are ten more Beatles songs on the record, just waiting for me to discover them. On the way home, my mother stops at my favorite Italian restaurant, Pal Joey's on Forest Avenue, to pick up takeout for dinner. She has ordered fried chicken for me, with a side of ziti.

Normally, fried chicken and ziti from Pal Joey's would be enough to make my night. But tonight, I just wish we could skip dinner and head straight home. I have an appointment with John, Paul, George, and—especially—Ringo.

11. And You Thought Thanksgiving Was Weird

By the time Christmas vacation rolls around, I really need it. My family celebrates Hanukkah, and on the first night I get a small rectangular box to open from my parents. Most years, Lissa and I sneak around when our parents aren't home and find all our gifts ahead of time, but this package is a surprise because it was already wrapped by the time we dug it up from behind all the shoes on the floor of our parents' bedroom closet.

It's a metronome! It is the kind that looks like a little radio, and it comes with a battery and a little earplug that attaches to it by a thin cord. Now I can find out what these things are for! I quickly put the plug in my ear, jam the battery into the compartment on the back of the metronome, and turn the volume dial on top until the thing clicks on. In my ear, there is a steady succession of TOCK-TOCK-TOCK noises, like someone banging a stick on a block of wood. I turn the other dial that is next to the volume control, which says TEMPO and has a bunch of tiny numbers around it, and the rhythm of the clicks gets faster and faster. Then I turn the knob the other way, and the clicks get slower and slower. I guess *tempo* means something like speed.

My parents are staring at me eagerly. "Wow, thank you! This is exactly what I wanted!" I say. I try to sound extremely excited, but I am not sure it totally works. I hadn't exactly understood what a metronome was for, but now I know.

Woo-hoo. I am the proud owner of a clicking machine.

Then Lissa opens her present, which is a shiny new pair of custom-made ice skates. New skates are a big deal for her, because she is a competitive figure skater. I have spent two or three afternoons a week at one of her training rinks since I was a little kid. My favorite is War Memorial Rink on Staten Island, because it is right near our house, and because I am great pals with Louie, the skate rental man. He is an old guy who was in the navy during World War II. I sit on top of the railing in front of the rental booth that's there to keep people lined up, and he tells me amazing stories about

D-Day while he smokes cigarettes and sharpens skates on the big machine behind the counter. The machine is very complicated. It has several spinning wheels attached to it. There is a cross-grinder for getting the blades flat and shiny, and a couple of different finishing wheels for hollowing out the bottoms of the blades and putting a sharp edge on them. It is the coolest thing ever! Sparks from the machine fly all around Louie's head the whole time, but he never stops talking or smoking.

In third grade, I did a project on Greek mythology, and one of my favorite Greek gods was Hephaestus, the god of the forge. He made all the weapons for the other gods. Louie reminds me of the illustration of Hephaestus in one of the books I used, because Hephaestus worked with flames and sparks all around him.

Louie has power. He controls fire. But he also has skill and craftsmanship. When he is turning a dull blade into a perfectly razor-sharp one, he pauses once in a while to run his calloused fingers along its edge. If he feels even the tiniest nick, he mumbles to himself, fires up the sharpener again, and touches just that little spot to the spinning wheel. He is never satisfied until the blade is perfect.

If I were Louie, I would be a war hero *and* I would be great at something.

Anyway, Lissa's professional-level skates are super expensive. They are custom-made to fit only her feet. They are fancier than anything I own. But this year, she doesn't look very excited as she thanks my parents. I don't get it, because if I were as good at something as Lissa is at skating, I would love to have the best equipment for it.

Like a big, shiny drum set with lots of flashing cymbals everywhere. That would be amazing.

Next, my dad opens a box from my mom. Inside are three ties. I sometimes have to wear a tie if we go to a wedding or something, and I hate it. Wearing a tie feels like choking to death. Very slowly. My dad looks pleased, though. He even kisses my mom, which causes me and Lissa to make faces at each other.

The only person left is my mom. Lissa gives her a painting she made in middle school art class. It's pretty good. Lissa is like my mom, because they are both excellent at art. I can tell my mom likes the present because she gives my sister a very long hug.

But then—disaster! My mom turns to my father and me. But we don't have anything to give her. We have been asking her what she wants for at least the past month, but all she ever says is "I don't need anything. I appreciate you every day, and I don't need a present to know you love me." So, for the first time ever, we haven't bought her a present.

When she realizes she isn't getting anything, my mother gives my father a super-mean look and bursts into tears. I try to hug her, but she doesn't hug me back. It is awful! I say, "Mom, you *told* us not to get you anything, so we *didn't* get you anything."

She sniffles a few times and then says, "You were supposed

to know. At least, your *father* was supposed to know." She says *father* like it is a dirty word.

As Lissa and I are on our way upstairs to our rooms, I ask her what I have done wrong. My mother told me not to do something, and I listened.

"You are so *stupid*," Lissa says.

I sit on the carpet floor of my bedroom for the longest time after that, holding my metronome but not knowing how to use it. Through the heat vent that leads from the kitchen into my closet, I can hear my parents arguing. For hours.

It is just another example of how following directions can drown you.

For the next few days, I just kind of mope around the house. Being the World's Worst Son isn't easy. Well, apparently, I have a natural gift for it, but it isn't *fun*. My dad and I go out to the Staten Island Mall and buy my mom a box of expensive chocolates and a scarf. The next night, each of us hands her one of the gifts. Again, she bursts into sobs.

I make a mental note that next year I should try to spend Hanukkah in Florida with my grandparents.

The morning after New Year's Eve, I wake up late and cross my room to Hecky's cage to say good morning. But it is not a good morning for Hecky, because both of her babies are curled up in the corner of the aquarium, dead.

I don't understand it. I have done everything the pet store

guy told me to do for them. I have fed them cut-up worms from our backyard every few days. I have turned on the heat lamp in their cage every morning and turned it off before going to bed each night. I have changed the water in the bowl more often than ever before. I have tried to spend some time holding them each day.

It doesn't matter. I have killed Hecky's babies.

I rush into Lissa's room to make sure Stripe is still all right. He is, and I take him out of his aquarium, which is right next to the one where she keeps her hamster, Freddy the Second. I try to do all of this quietly, because she is still asleep, but the clicking of the clips on the cage lid wakes her up. She starts to yell at me for waking her up but stops when she realizes I am crying.

"What's wrong, Jord?" she asks. But I can't even get the words out. All that comes from my throat is a horrible squeaking noise. Lissa gets out of bed and puts her arms around me. I sit there for the longest time, just trying to keep Stripe warm and comfortable against my shaking chest.

I thought what I wanted for Hanukkah was a drum, but I was wrong. I shouldn't have wished for anything that comes in a package. What I really wish is that I could stop ruining everything, and maybe even be *particularly good* at something.

12. My Rotten Brain

Well, Hanukkah might have been depressing, but Presidents' Day does its best to cheer me up by dumping more than a foot of snow and canceling a day of school. I need the break, too, for two reasons. Ever since Christmas, everybody's baby snakes have been dying off. Steven's went at the very beginning of January, followed by one of B.J.'s, both of Peter's, one of Robert's, the second one of B.J.'s, and then the second of Robert's. Now the only two left aside from Stripe are the ones at Jonah Carp's house.

Also, Mrs. Fisher has gone completely off the rails.

As usual, it all started because of something that wasn't my fault. There is a big group of kids in my class who are having a lot of trouble with reading, so every day, Mrs. Fisher takes them to a table in the back and works with them on phonics. She gives the rest of us work to do, but the work is way too easy. We are supposed to get cards out of the SRA reading kit if we finish early during these times, but those are easy, too. It only takes me maybe five minutes to read a card and answer all the questions in my head. After that, because I am trying really hard to be good, I have been reading silently. Every day, I bring in something interesting, because I know I am going to be spending a lot of time with it.

And that's where the trouble starts: Mrs. Fisher and I have different ideas of what makes an interesting book. She says science fiction is "trash." Fantasy is "junk." My all-time favorite book, *Bad Luck Stars of Sports*, is "all right, if you like that kind of thing."

All right if you like that kind of thing? It's *only* the most important book I have ever read. Without it, I wouldn't have learned about my hero and role model, Ron Hunt—the coolest baseball player ever. He holds the all-time record for getting hit by the pitch. He once got hit fifty times in a single

HALL OF FAME

HANK AARON

RON GUIDRY

season! Sure, Babe Ruth was the first and biggest baseball star. Hank Aaron has the most homers in history. There are guys with more stolen bases, more runs batted in, and more runs scored. There are a million better fielders, and we haven't even mentioned pitchers yet. Ron Guidry, the Yankees' best pitcher, went twenty-five and three this year, and is the best fielder I have ever seen in my life.

But nobody has more guts than Ron Hunt. He's the toughest. And that is why he is my role model. I am a terrible hitter, because my parents always take me to the eye doctor in September, so by April my glasses prescription isn't strong enough. It is hard to *hit* the ball if you can't *see* it. Still, thanks to Ron Hunt, I have a new plan for the 1979 Little League

BABE RUTH

RON HUNT

season: I am going to get hit by the pitch as much as possible.

It is totally foolproof. I don't have to have any talent to get beaned. I just need the courage of Ron Hunt.

I did my last book report on *Bad Luck Stars of Sports* so Mrs. Fisher could learn what a great book it is, but she didn't give me an *Excellent*, like William Feranek got. On the front cover of the report, right over the picture of Ron Hunt that I had spent hours drawing, she wrote *GOOD* in gigantic letters.

GOOD is bad.

When I opened up the report and saw Mrs. Fisher's comments, I saw that all she had written—in huge red letters across my words—was, *Sloppy work. You were supposed to skip lines. In the future, you must follow directions!* This was the dumbest thing ever! I made the report three pages long without skipping lines, and it was supposed to be three pages long *with* skipping lines. So I wrote twice as much as everybody else about a completely life-changing book and got yelled at in red for it.

That was when I decided something. If Mrs. Fisher was just going to hate me and whatever I read, I might as well not care anymore. So I started to bring comic books to school. I knew she would hate them, but I also knew she would be wrong. Comic books have excellent lessons. Along with Spider-Man's motto, "With great power comes great responsibility," I have learned tons of other things from other comics. I mean, just last summer, in *DC Comics Limited Collector's Edition*

#55: *The Millennium Massacre*, Superboy and the Legion of Super-Heroes taught me love is more important than war. The X-Men have always taught me that you can't judge people just for being different from you. Then there are the Avengers, Earth's Mightiest Heroes. They have taught me that you have to stick up for your friends, no matter what.

Meanwhile, two seats away, Britt Stone is reading a million books about snotty girls and their horses. What is she going to learn from them? She is already exceptionally good at being a snotty girl who rides horses.

Anyway, the last day before Presidents' Day weekend, Mrs. Fisher comes storming over to my desk and interrupts my reading of the excellent *Avengers #182: The Many Faces of Evil*. I'm thinking, *Do you mind? I'm about to learn the secret origins of the Scarlet Witch and her brother, Quicksilver.* But I am smart enough not to say that.

"JORR-dan!" she says. "You are *supposed* to be **reading!**"

I bite my lip to stop myself from saying, "Then it's a good thing I *am* reading!" Instead, I just sit there with the comic in my hands.

"But instead, you are wasting valuable class time with these . . . **comic books!**"

Now I have to say something. "I'm not wasting time. I learn a lot from comic books!"

She snorts at me. What kind of teacher *snorts* at her students?

"What could you possibly learn from . . . *that*?"

I tell myself to stay calm, because I don't want my mom to

get a call reminding her about how doomed my future is. Plus, now the whole class is staring at me.

"Well," I say serenely, "for one thing, there is excellent vocabulary in comic books. Look, just on the first page of this one, there's, umm, *united*. And *withstand*. And *degenerative*. And *ceased*. And *thy*."

"I bet you don't even know what those words mean!" Mrs. Fisher snarls.

I am dying to say, "If this class *united*, we could *withstand* the *degenerative* effects of having you for a teacher, and band together until *thy* reign of terror *ceased*!" Instead, I just say, "Yes, I do. *United* means—"

"I know what *united* means, JORR-dan! Now, put that thing away and find something else to read. If I see you with another comic book, I will confiscate it!"

Hey, I know what *confiscate* means. Thanks to comic books.

"Do you understand me?" she barks.

"Yes," I say, staring directly into her beady witch eyes.

"Good. Because comic books will rot your brain!"

In that case, I'm thinking Mrs. Fisher must have read a whole lot of comic books.

So you can see why I needed this longer-than-usual Presidents' Day break. It doesn't turn out the way I would have hoped, though. Friday is our first day off, and I am all excited to sleep late. Unfortunately, my mother wakes me up frantically before it is even eight o'clock.

"Get up, Jord!" she shouts. "Your snake is missing!"

I jump out of bed, grab my glasses, and rush over to Hecky's cage, where she is happily curled around the fresh new tree branch I just put in there last week.

"What are you talking about, Mom?" I say. "Hectoria is right here."

"Not that snake. Your *other* one!"

Stripe.

I dash across the hall to Lissa's room and peer into his cage. She is right: He is gone. This doesn't make any sense at all. Over the years, Lissa and I have dealt with a lot of pet escapes. The original Freddy the Hamster was a breakout expert, and the snake I had before Hecky once got out of his cage by crawling up the side and then pushing the lid up with his head. But the new aquarium tanks we have come with snap clips on the lids so you can't open them just by pushing up. Plus, Stripe is still only something like seven inches long, and he lives in a cage with twelve-inch-tall walls and no climbing stick.

But Lissa, who is standing there, says, "You know what this means, Jord? A *pet hunt*!" She smiles at me, because we both secretly love pet hunts. My mother freaks out the whole time there is a pet on the loose, but for us, it is a great adventure every time. When we are on a pet-finding mission, we don't even fight.

If my parents were smart, they would let Hecky or Freddy the Second out once a day.

Anyway, we know the routine. First, we go through the

junk drawer downstairs to get the most important piece of pet-tracking equipment: flashlights! These are necessary because snakes and hamsters always go right for the darkest places in the house. Usually, we find the missing animal under a radiator, smushed into the back of a closet, or way in the corner of a room, under somebody's bed.

Once, we even found the original Freddy asleep in one of my mom's high-heeled shoes. Now my mom has a special rack in her closet to keep all her footwear off the ground.

As soon as we have the flashlights in hand, we split up. Because I am smaller and better at getting my head way down low, I am on Radiator Duty. Because she is bigger and lazier, Lissa is the Closet Inspector. I check in my room first, but there is nothing under either of my heaters. Lissa's room is harder, because there are piles of clothing and junk blocking one radiator, and the other is behind her desk. When I squeeze my way under the desk, I can't quite get my head down far enough to see because there is a wooden foot rail in the way. I have to twist my arm almost upside down and then feel around with the back of my hand. I find a bunch of dust and twenty-eight cents, but no baby snake.

Meanwhile, Lissa has already checked out both our bedrooms and the upstairs bathroom, which is past Lissa's door and around the corner between our house's two extremely creepy attics. I hand her the twenty-eight cents, and we head downstairs. Our mom follows us around making alarmed noises, which get louder and louder the closer we get to her bedroom closet. We don't find Stripe anywhere. All that is left to check is the basement.

And the attics, which are definitely the last place anybody would want to check. First of all, there is stuff piled up everywhere in them. They make Lissa's room look like a model of clean living. Second of all, it is freezing and scary in those attics. Besides, I don't think any sane snake would hide in either of them in the winter, because snakes are cold-blooded, which means they need to stay warm to survive.

We go downstairs first. When Lissa opens the basement door, Spicy is waiting there on the top step. He sleeps in the basement, where we keep his litter box, but he is almost always ready on the steps to pounce on whichever person comes to let him out of there and feed him in the morning. I expect him to rush past Lissa to his food bowl, which is on a floor mat in front of the kitchen sink. But he doesn't. He follows us down.

That's when I start to panic. Why isn't Spicy hungry? He's always hungry when we come downstairs. What if he has *already eaten*?

While Lissa goes around the basement checking closets, I crouch down in front of Spicy and check out his paws. I don't see any blood on them, which might be a good sign. But maybe it just means he is a neat eater. I am almost shivering with fear as I hold Spicy still with one hand and push his lips back from his teeth with the other. Usually, Spicy goes nuts and starts scratching if you try to touch his face. Oh, who am I kidding? Usually, Spicy goes nuts and starts scratching if you get anywhere near him. But he drapes himself calmly over my arm as I put my face right up to his and look at his mouth.

No blood there, either.

The basement looks like a dead end. Lissa looks at me. "Attic?" she asks.

A shudder runs through me. "Attic," I reply.

But on our way up there, Lissa stops in her room to put socks on. I follow her and decide to check Stripe's cage more closely. I basically shove my whole head inside and look everywhere. I even lift up the two miniature bowls we have in there: one for Stripe's drinking water and one for the chunks of earthworm I have been feeding him. I don't find any hint of anything.

It's almost like the snake has disappeared.

I am just about to get up when I hear a strange sound. It's kind of like somebody is crumpling up paper into balls. Or breaking very small twigs.

Or *munching*. I look into Freddy the Second's cage and almost throw up. The hamster is standing up on his back paws, holding his front ones up to his face. I peer around the enclosure, and there are half-inch black-and-red sections of what looks like a strangely colored pencil everywhere. I take an even closer look at Freddy the Second's hands, and see that he is holding something in them.

Something with eyeballs.

"Lissa!" I yell.

"What?" she says in her smart-big-sister voice. "And why are you shouting? I'm right here."

In a weird voice that doesn't even sound like mine, I mumble, "I found Stripe."

So my sister is a murderer. The only thing we can figure out is that she "accidentally" put Stripe in the wrong cage after she played with him last night. At least, she swears she did it "accidentally." I tell her I am going to accidentally punch her, but my mom stops me. In our family, the only punishment for killing your little brother's pet in cold blood is that your father says he is "disappointed" because you "have been an irresponsible pet owner."

Ooh, that ought to teach her!

I don't talk to Lissa the whole rest of the weekend, even after my mom points out that I once forgot to feed Freddie the Second for a whole week while Lissa was at skating camp. I don't care. Forgetting to feed a pet is totally different from *feeding one pet to your other pet*!

Thank God the last two babies are safe at Jonah Carp's house. His dad is a scientist, and they have tons and tons of animals, from his older brother's boa constrictor to his older sister's rabbits to the three turtles that live in their upstairs hall. If anybody knows how to keep reptiles alive, it's the Carps.

On Monday, Presidents' Day, it snows more than a foot! That means we are off from school on Tuesday. Jonah calls me on Tuesday morning to see whether I want to walk the mile to his house, because he has an excellent snow day plan. His brother is taking apart and rebuilding a 1960s Volkswagen Beetle, and Jonah wants to drag the car's hood down the street from his house to Dead Man's Hill, the best sledding spot on the whole island. Jonah is pretty sure we can turn the hood upside down and use it as a five-person sleigh.

That's so crazy it just might work!

My mom doesn't want me to walk all the way to Jonah's house in the snow, but I convince her that it is good exercise. She must feel really sorry for me after the recent snake homicide, because she says she will walk over there with me and spend the afternoon hanging out with Mrs. Carp. Walking a mile each way in a foot of snow is SUPER exhausting, but the sledding is unbelievable!

Okay, it turns out that you can't actually steer an upside-down car hood as it is zooming down a hill with five boys trying desperately not to fly off it. You can go incredibly fast, though, and laugh as all the single sledders have to swerve to avoid getting flattened by your massive Sled of Doom. We have so much fun doing this that I forget all about Hecky's last two babies until sundown forces us to head back to Jonah's house.

I ask Jonah if I can visit the baby snakes, and he says very casually, "Oh, I forgot to tell you—they died a month ago. How are the other ones doing?"

I decide two things right then and there.

Number one is that I can't trust anybody.

Number two is that I will never love anything again.

13. The Almost-Last Straw

By the end of February, everything is depressing. Mrs. Fisher is worse than ever, and now it is even making my parents fight. One night, after I go up to bed, I hear them snapping at each other downstairs in the kitchen. I tiptoe over to my closet and climb up on the shelf next to the heat vent to listen.

"Carol, if we move him to another school, what are we teaching him?" my father asks. "We don't want him to think he can just quit whenever life gets difficult."

"Harv, his teacher hates him. She really *hates* him."

"I think that is an exaggeration, honey."

"No, it isn't. You weren't at the parent conference. You didn't see her face when she said he would never amount to anything. I did."

For the first time ever, sitting there in my closet, I start pulling hairs out of my head when my mother isn't even at her night class. It's one thing to feel like my teacher hates me. It's another thing to hear my mom say it as a fact.

"Maybe you should cut back on your night classes for a

while. It seems that Jordan's behavior is worse when you take this many."

"I can't just cut back on my classes, Harv. I'm in the middle of the semester! Maybe *you* can cut back on doing rounds at the nursing home at night."

"You know that is not an option. My patients need me."

Oh boy. They can go on and on about this for hours. My father hates my mom's PhD program. He thinks it's her job to be at home with Lissa and me. But he works a million hours a week, so we only really get to spend time with him on Friday nights and Sundays.

On Friday nights, my father takes Lissa and me to Baskin-Robbins for sundaes. On Sunday mornings, we go out to one of the little stores that sell newspapers, and Dad gets the *New York Times*. He always lets me buy three comics. Three is the limit, because he is trying to teach me to be responsible with money.

But that isn't working, because my mom takes me to a different store on Saturdays and lets me buy more.

Maybe it's none of my business, but I think maybe my parents need to work on their communication skills.

I start to fall asleep right there on the shelf as they drone on at each other. But my head snaps back up when my mother says, "Harvey, that's IT! Tomorrow, I am talking to Joan Purow about P.S. 54. AND I am calling the board of ed to see what it would take to get a transfer. At least then we'll know what the *option* looks like."

"I still think you're being hasty with this."

"Of course you do! This is just like what happened with your arm!"

What happened with my dad's arm? I have no idea. But I guess he knows what my mom means, because he says, "I don't know what you want from me! I've already made the appointment with Dr. Suarez."

"That's great, Harv. But I feel like I have to push you for three months every time there's a problem. If we wait three months for this, Jordan's year will be over and the damage will be done! I'm calling Joan in the morning."

"Fine! But can we please see whether Jordan wants to move before we make a decision?"

Oh, yikes! I don't want to switch schools in the middle of the year. At least, I don't *think* I do. I have been at P.S. 35 my whole life. I have friends at P.S. 35. I know what to expect at P.S. 35. I like our traditions, like having grade-wide kickball tournaments twice a year and decorating the maypole every spring. I know the school song:

> *The Clove Valley School, we'll always remember you,*
> *The teachers that we had, and all the lessons, too,*
> *To learn to spell, to read and write,*
> *Learning what's wrong and learning what's right!*

Come to think of it, the song is pretty dumb. But still, I don't want to leave. That's like letting Mrs. Fisher win.

She's the one who should leave.

On the other hand, B.J. has been my best friend since

preschool. In fact, his real name is Benjamin, but everybody calls him B.J. because when we were three years old, all the kids in our class had trouble pronouncing his name—which means I've known him since before I could even talk right. Maybe it would be okay to be in class with him. Also, he's even smarter than William Feranek. If other kids in his class are that smart, maybe I won't be so bored with how slow things are, like I am now. And Peter Friedman is in fifth grade there, so I would probably see him around sometimes.

On the *other* other hand, Louise Boily said I'm not zee kind of boy who lets go of zee rope. And running away from my mean teacher feels like letting go of zee rope.

I don't know how long I sit there, but eventually, my parents stop arguing and my mom stomps out of the kitchen. Then she starts walking up the stairs. I know she is about to peek into my room to check on me!

I rush back to my bed and dive under the covers just in time. Mom stands in the doorway for ages. I can tell because I hear her breathing, and because her body is blocking the shaft of light from the hallway that usually crosses my bedroom floor. When she finally goes back down the stairs, I realize my hands are clenched into fists.

And my left hand is grasping a big clump of hair.

For the next few days, I feel like I am having an asthma attack every second. I am in such a panic that I can't breathe right. I have a bald spot! It's on the left side of my head, above and just in front of my ear. Every morning when I wake up, I rush to the bathroom and twist my head to the side to look at it. The hair doesn't show any signs of growing back.

Now I am not just an obstreperous boy who can't pay attention in class, or a terrible pet owner who lets all his snake's babies die, or the third-shortest kid in my grade. Now I am the first kid ever to go bald before his tenth birthday. And I did this to myself. I am a *freak*.

Forget about sending me to a different school. My parents should probably just ship me off to the circus.

At school, I keep holding my breath, waiting for some-body to say something about the baldness. The only thing in the world I have to be thankful for is that the spot is on the left side of my head, and Britt Stone sits on my right side.

Things have gotten as bad as they possibly can with Mrs. Fisher, too. Now that I am not allowed to read comics, I am even more bored. I finish reading the last of the dark purple SRA cards, and then I have absolutely nothing to do, so I begin to find little art projects to keep me busy.

Basically, this consists of making little glue men inside my desk.

It's easy and fun! Here's how it works: First, I take my container of Elmer's Glue-All and carefully make a glue out-line of a man on the metal bottom of my desk drawer. In about ten minutes, when the outline is dry enough that I don't get any glue on me if I poke it, I fill in the middle by pouring a puddle of glue until the whole inside of the man is covered. About half an hour after that, when the middle is dry enough to touch, but not dry enough to get stiff or brittle, I carefully peel the glue man up off the bottom of the drawer.

If everything goes right, he's like a stretchy little puppet and I can use him to play superheroes in my desk until Mrs. Fisher is finally done with the slow readers at the back table.

Robert starts a glue man factory inside his desk, too, and this is even better. Now we can have superhero *battles* in our laps! If he holds his glue men down between his knees, I can see them from across the room.

Unfortunately, we get too involved in the pretend battle one day and don't notice that Mrs. Fisher has come to stand behind me.

"JORR-dan!" she thunders.

Why is it always JORR-dan? ROBB-ert is sitting ten feet away with his hands covered in Elmer's—how about yelling at him for a little change of pace?

I look up.

"WHY are you not working on an SRA card like the rest of the children who have finished their work?"

Again, is Robert invisible or something?

"I've read all the SRA cards," I explain. "I'm done with the whole box!"

"You're lying," Mrs. Fisher says, marching over to the file

cabinet above the cards. She opens one of the drawers, snatches out a tan folder, looks inside, and says, "HAH!" Then she marches back over to me as the whole class stares. "Look at your folder," she says triumphantly.

Folder? I didn't know I had a folder.

"Every one of the answer sheets in here is blank! You have not read a single SRA card all year!"

Answer sheets? I guess that's the part of the instructions I missed. But still, I have read every card, and I've done all the answers in my head. Plus, now I am mad and embarrassed, so I say, "I have read *every* SRA card!"

She bends down so her nose is inches from mine and says, "I don't believe you."

"I know every answer for every card. I can prove it. Go ahead—pick a card! Pick a *dark purple* card."

She looks around at the class and hisses, "Get back to work, CHILL-dren!" Then she stomps over to the box and grabs a few cards. She asks me each of the five questions on the back of the first card, and I tell her each answer before she can even begin to read me the multiple-choice options.

Hey, I am particularly good at something after all! I have a great memory.

Mrs. Fisher goes through two more cards with me before she believes it: I know all the answers, just like I said. And she is not happy about it.

"Well, JORR-dan," she sneers. "Now you will go back to the beginning of the box and write . . . down . . . the answer . . . to every . . . single . . . question!"

Then she grabs my Elmer's Glue-All and slams it into one of her desk drawers.

14. The Slap

My last day at P.S. 35 feels all wrong from the start. On the way to school, my mother asks me if I want to transfer to P.S. 54, and I feel like I am going to either faint or throw up. I pretend I haven't heard the question, and concentrate on playing paradiddles with my hands on the tops of my legs.

"Jordan, are you going to answer me?" she says.

"Right-left-right-right, left-right-left-left," I say to myself.

She repeats what she said, but I just keep slapping away. A great new song called "Heart of Glass" by a lady named Blondie is playing on the radio, and I try to focus on playing my paradiddles in time with the beat. It's really hard! If I think too much about the beat, I mess up the hand pattern. If I think too much about the hand pattern, I lose the beat. But if I forget about both the hand pattern and the beat, and just play without thinking, everything melts away but the music. I almost get there, but then I mess up. I take a deep breath and start over. Once again, I feel like I am just at the edge of becoming part of the song.

Then my mom shuts off the radio.

"Honey, I'm not trying to pressure you. I just hate watching you suffer."

"I don't know," I whine. How am I supposed to make such a big decision? I can't even be responsible for a bunch of baby snakes. Who says I should be in charge of the Decision Department? *I* hate watching me suffer, too. But what if B.J.'s teacher is just as mean as Mrs. Fisher? What if she's *meaner*?

"Well, just think about it, all right? Your father and I will support whatever decision you make."

That doesn't feel true to me at all. My father will support me if I decide to stay. My mother will support me if I decide to go. It's all just a big, gigantic, stupid mess. I'm a kid! All I should have to worry about is how the Yankees are going to look this season now that they have traded Sparky Lyle, my favorite relief pitcher. Or whether my mom and dad will ever buy me a snare drum of my own.

I almost wish somebody would just make the choice for me.

I turn the radio back on. The Blondie song is over, and "September" by Earth, Wind & Fire is playing. It's too slow for paradiddles.

That figures. Now my musical breakthrough is ruined, and I will never, ever get decent at playing drums.

Or dictionaries. Laps. Whatever.

When my mom drops me off, I drag my feet all the way up the sidewalk, all the way up the stairs, and all the way down the long hall to the cafeteria to line up with my class. There are already four boys in front of me—with William Feranek right in front. He always gets to school first, because he lives just around the corner, and also because it is yet another sign of how perfect he is. I line up behind Kenneth. Britt Stone is fifth in the girls' line, so we are standing only a couple of inches apart.

"*Hi*, Jordan," she says in a fake, sweet voice, blinking her eyes at me several times. I hate when Britt talks to me in that voice. It makes me feel like I am blushing, and also nervous. I know if I say hi back, she will laugh and then start teasing me about something. But if I don't say hi back, then she will tell me how unfriendly I am.

Like basically everything else in my life, this is a trap.

I ignore her and start tapping out a double stroke roll on the outsides of my hips. "Ma-ma-da-da, ma-ma-da-da," I whisper, settling into a rhythm that isn't fast enough to mess me up.

"Mama! Dada!" Britt purrs in my ear. "Ooh, what's wrong, little baby?" I lose the beat completely. I glare at her.

"Shut up, *Brat* Stone!" Oh, that's a good one! I will have to remember—

"No, *you* shut up, Baldy!" she snaps.

My heart stops. I whip my head around to see whether anybody else is listening, but it looks as though nobody is paying attention. Still, this is my worst nightmare. Britt Stone knows I am bald. My life is ruined! I stare down at my feet so she won't see the tears in my eyes, and she doesn't say anything else.

Why should she? She has already defeated me for life.

Miss Janet comes and leads us upstairs to room 4-210. I don't look at anybody. Britt could be staring at me! Or worse, other kids could be staring at me. Has she told them about my bald spot? Or have they noticed on their own? *What if everybody knows*, and Britt is just the only kid mean enough to say it to my face?

I sit down and put my face in my hands. Everything is spinning around in my head at once. Paradiddles. Double stroke rolls. My mom saying, *Honey, I'm not trying to pressure you*, while she is pressuring me. Britt Stone saying, *Baldy*. I can't make the thoughts stop!

Then, suddenly, Mrs. Fisher is grabbing me by the front of my shirt and yanking me to my feet. Her face is clenched up in terrifying fury. What have I done? I look around and see that everybody else in the class is standing with their hands over their hearts.

Somehow, I have managed to ignore the Pledge of Allegiance.

"You'll stand up for your COUNTRY and your GOD!" my teacher shouts.

The words come flying out of me before I can even think about them. "Any God that would let *you* teach children—"

SMACK! Mrs. Fisher has slapped me across the face.

I have gotten my wish. Somebody has made the decision for me. Just like that, I have no choice but to let go of zee rope.

15. Miss Tuff

My mom keeps me home the day after The Slap, and spends hours on the phone arranging for me to start at P.S. 54 the next day. I am basically in shock. First of all, my teacher *hit me*. Second of all, now she's not my teacher anymore. I never have to see Mrs. Fisher or Britt Stone again! But this also means I won't see Robert Falcone every day, or Steven Vitale. I won't pass Jonah Carp in the halls, or get to smile at my first-grade teacher, Mrs. Gross, on the way to lunch.

And I won't know anything. I won't know my way around the building. I won't know the schedule, or how the lunch line works. I won't know which aides are nice and which ones are mean. I won't even know who the principal is! I mean, the principal of P.S. 35, Mrs. Coseglia, wasn't nice—in fact, I was terrified of her. But at least she wasn't a *mystery*.

Plus, what if B.J. acts different when his school friends are around? What if Peter Friedman ignores me because he is a big fifth grader and doesn't associate with fourth graders? What if none of the kids in my new class like me? What if they all notice my bald spot on the very first day and decide

I am a weird nut? What if they find out I had to leave my old school because I am *so bad that my teacher hit me*?

To top it all off, after my mom's last phone call, she tells me I am going to be in B.J.'s class, and that my new teacher is named Miss Tough. I am thinking, *Are you kidding me? My last teacher hit me, and my new teacher is named Miss Tough?* It sounds like a joke, but I don't find it funny due to the fact that it is actually my *life*.

That night I can't sleep. It is Wednesday, which means my mother is at Rutgers. I start to panic about what is going to happen in the morning, and my chest feels so tight that I have to get up and do two puffs of my inhaler. Then I lie in bed, shaking and pulling hairs out of my head, until I hear my mom's car pull into our driveway.

Great! The only thing worse than being a bald, bad new kid is being a *balder*, bad new kid who has barely slept.

The drive to P.S. 54 takes for*ever*. It's so strange—the route takes us right past P.S. 35. My heart starts to beat really hard when I look at the top right corner of the building at Mrs. Fisher's window. I have to tell myself over and over, *She can't hit you now, she can't hit you now*, until we are on the highway and Mrs. Fisher is just a fading spot in the rearview mirror.

Ten minutes later, my mom parks her Chevy Nova in front of my new school. The place is huge! There are three stories instead of two, plus there's even a basement! There's a fancy front porch with an overhang like movie theaters have, with a marble entrance arch around the entryway. When we get inside and meet with the assistant principal, Mr. Levy, he tells us there are five classes in each grade. P.S. 35 only had two classes per grade, so coming here feels like moving to a bigger, busier city. I don't know what he has heard about me, but he must have heard something, because as he is walking me upstairs to class, he says, "This is your chance to make a fresh, clean start, Jordan. Make it count, all right?"

A fresh, clean start sounds good. On the other hand, I am pretty sure my new assistant principal thinks I am going to be trouble.

When Mr. Levy stops at room 303, I have just enough time to read the nameplate on the door before he knocks. It says, MISS TUFF.

Maybe if it isn't spelled *Tough*, she isn't mean. But what do I know? I have literally been wrong about every teacher I've ever met.

Miss Tuff answers the door and smiles warmly at me.

It's a trick! a little voice says in the corner of my mind.

"Oh, you must be Jordan," she says. "Benjamin has told me all about you!"

Ooh, she's good, says the little voice.

"Class, this is our new friend Jordan," Miss Tuff says, leading me into the room and stopping in front of the chalkboard. "Jordan, why don't you introduce yourself?"

I look at her. I am confused. She just told everybody my name. What else does she expect me to say?

"You don't have to tell us a whole lot. Just things like your name and where you are joining us from."

I'm thinking, *My name is Jordan Sonnenblick, and I am fleeing the violence of P.S. 35.*

But I just say, "Hi, I'm Jordan. Uh, P.S. 35." Then I shuffle my feet and blush, because I sound like a moron.

Miss Tuff says, "We are so glad to have you, Jordan!" She puts her arm around me, and her hand brushes against the left side of my head, where the bald spot is.

I can't help it—I *flinch*. Miss Tuff feels me pull away from her, and as the class gets back to whatever work I have interrupted, she says softly in my ear, "Oh, you don't like being touched? I promise I will remember that."

Tears spring up in my eyes. I *love* being touched. My mom has always referred to me as her "affectionate child." But I am afraid of being touched by a teacher, because The Slap happened two days ago. And I am even more afraid my bald spot will be discovered. I look up and sideways at Miss Tuff. She must see that I am nearly crying, because she says, "Don't worry. You are going to be happy here!"

That's when I start to feel just the tiniest bit of hope in my heart. Miss Tuff is not tough.

The other kids in my class are wildly different from the kids at P.S. 35. There are five other Jewish students! And the other kids aren't all Catholic, like nearly everybody at my old school. There are kids whose families come from all over Asia, with amazing names that feel like tongue twisters in my mouth: Chandra Mahapaurya, Ramesh Ganeshram, Mondhipa Ratnarathorn. Also, the boys aren't only interested in sports. During recess, B.J. introduces Jonathan Marks by saying he is a "chess genius." Jonathan's opponent, a tall, thin, serious-looking kid with a deep voice, introduces himself as "Walter P. Kelly." That sounds very sophisticated. I mean, my middle name is Ted, but I have never called myself "Jordan T. Sonnenblick." "Walter P. Kelly" is a grown-up name, like he should already be a doctor. Or a tough, no-nonsense detective: "Walter P. Kelly, Private Eye." B.J. sits down to play against a small, frizzy-haired boy named Stuart Heffer, who tells me he is in the middle of a massive project. Stuart wants to be the first kid ever to read the entire *World Book Encyclopedia* by his eleventh birthday. Last summer, he read the entire *B* volume!

I'm like, *Well, I read several extremely informative comic books last summer.* But somehow, I get the feeling Stuart is way ahead of me in the information department.

The girls are all really serious about school. Stephanie Casella and Laura LoBianco both want to be lawyers when they grow up, and there are tons of others who say they are going to be doctors someday. At P.S. 35, I never heard anybody talk about what they were going to be when they grew up.

I am impressed, but also a bit scared. I had thought it would be exciting to be in a class with a lot of intelligent kids, but it never occurred to me that if everybody else was smarter, it might make me look dumber in comparison. In my other school, I was "that smart kid who gets in trouble all the time." What if in my new school, I am just "that kid who gets in trouble all the time"?

By the end of the day, I am sure I like Miss Tuff. I also feel like I have a lot of new friends, even though the experience of being the new kid is overwhelming.

It isn't until the second day that my problems start. While I am laughing at lunch with B.J., Jonathan, and two really funny boys named Joey Chablis and Chuck Dai, I notice that a kid named Albert is glaring at me from my class's other table. When we go outside to play kickball, I am playing second base and he purposely steps on my foot as he is running from first to second. This hurts because he is nearly as big as Walter P. Kelly. I say, "What's your problem?"

"You think you're so hot, don't you?" Albert says. He looks really mad, and I have no idea what I have done.

"What are you talking about?"

"Stupid new kid! You took my seat at lunch."

I don't get it. All I did was take the last empty place at B.J.'s table. But I do not like getting accused. Or stepped on.

"Oh, yeah?" I spit. "I must have missed the big sign that said, 'For Buttheads Only.'"

"*You're* a butthead."

"Great comeback," I say. "Have you tried out for *Saturday Night Live* yet?"

Albert snarls, "That's it! You're dead!" Then a girl named

Samantha kicks the ball into the outfield, so Albert runs from second to third, and that ends our lively chat. But Albert stares at me the whole rest of the game.

I can't believe this! I haven't gotten in anything remotely resembling a fight at school since a bloody incident in second grade, when some new kid who had just moved to Staten Island from Vermont stabbed me in the hand with his scissors during art. And I hadn't actually done any fighting that time.

I mostly did the bleeding part.

And my two fights at camp were with other tiny guys like me. Fighting Albert is going to be like fighting a tree. I'm not even sure my fists will be able to reach all the way up to his face. But I know one thing for sure: I can't back down. If I do, Albert will just pick on me all year.

Fortunately, my father has given me some boxing lessons in our basement. He watches boxing matches on TV all the time. Plus, when he was a kid, he used to box with his older cousins in their basement. He calls boxing "the sweet science" and has taught me a lot about how it works. I know how to jab and uppercut. I know I have to keep moving my feet, but keep my body angled slightly sideways so I "present a smaller target." I know I have to keep my elbows in to protect my ribs, and my hands up so the other guy doesn't have a clear shot at my face.

And I am getting better and better. Just the other day, I hit my dad so hard he had to call time out and stop to rub his forearm. Then afterward, he even put ice on it.

The only thing I don't know about boxing is whether this stuff works in real life, when the enemy isn't (a) wearing padded gloves and (b) my dad.

The whole afternoon, I try to concentrate on Miss Tuff and our lessons so I won't get in trouble, but I am so nervous that she asks me twice to stop tapping my pencil against my desk. Actually, it's worse than that. *She* only asks me twice, but Stephanie Casella, who sits next to me, asks me at least *ten times*. Stephanie even catches me whistling "Drive My Car" when we are supposed to be reading silently.

This is perfect. Even if I survive the fight, now my teacher has noticed my problem with sitting still, and Stephanie probably thinks I am the most annoying kid in America.

When we are dismissed, I try to walk fast enough so I can get out to the area where my mom will pull up before Albert

can get to me. Unfortunately, when I am halfway there I find the entire sidewalk blocked by Albert, who has two other boys with him—one on each side.

This is ridiculous! It's just my luck that in my second day at a new school, I run into the only fourth grader in the world who has his own *henchmen*. I start to say, "I'm sorry I took your seat. I really didn't know it was yours." But all I get to say is "I'm—" before Albert steps toward me, puts both his hands on my chest, and shoves. I go flying backward, and the only thing that stops me from falling on my butt is that I reach back to catch myself, which makes me land on my metal lunch box instead.

Sadly, metal is harder than my butt. The edge of the lunch box smashes into my spine and I can't stop myself from letting out a weak little "Ow!"

All right, then. Now there's no way I can stop a fight from happening. (Or really, continuing.) But Albert is twice my size, and it's three against one. Thinking fast, I show him my lunch box. "Okay," I say. "Here's how this is gonna go. Either you let me pass, or I am going to hit you in the face with this lunch box."

He sneers. "You're not serious."

"Try me."

"Fine, I will," he says, but this time his voice doesn't sound so brave.

"Excellent!" I say as cheerfully as I can. I look down at the lunch box and pretend to study all the slightly raised NFL team helmet emblems on it. Then I add, "You're going to look great with a Pittsburgh Steelers flag–shaped dent in your forehead. Or you can step aside."

Albert's two sidekicks look at the lunch box, then at their leader. For a second, I think there is a chance of him backing down, but I realize he isn't going to let himself look bad in front of these guys.

Well, if I wait any longer for the action to start, either we are going to get in trouble with a teacher or—even worse—my mom is going to pull up beside us and see me misbehaving at my brand-new school. And Dad always says you should never let your opponent take the first shot. I cock my right fist down low around the handle of the lunch box and step forward. Albert raises his fists and starts to swing at me.

I swing as hard as I can. BONG! goes the lunch box. BONG! goes Albert's face. He stumbles backward, holding his nose.

"You hid me wig a lutch box!" he says, looking at me with hurt in his eyes. Like this had been some kind of surprise move on my part.

"Yup," I say, trying to sound like my heart isn't going a million miles an hour. "And tomorrow, I'm bringing my *big* lunch box!" I step around Albert, wondering whether his sidekicks are going to step in and block my path.

They move aside, and I don't blame them. They're probably concerned I might also be packing a thermos.

16. What the Heck IS a Three-Mile Island?

A couple of weeks later, I am sitting on my butt in the hallway, with all my classmates around me. Miss Tuff is telling us to "skootch your tushies into the wall." I have been through a lot of these atomic-bomb drills at P.S. 35, and I have always thought they were the dumbest thing ever. I live in New York City, okay? If atomic bombs start falling, I know we are going to get blown up before almost anywhere else. Plus, I have never understood how hiding in the hallway with my butt crunched into the crack between the wall and the floor is supposed to protect me from explosions or radiation. If a bomb did hit, the wall would just fall over right on top of me. And if that didn't get me, the wave of radiation would probably make me glow in the dark.

Briefly. Until it killed me.

So usually, I giggle my way through the drill. And that is how the kids around me have always behaved, too. Today, though, we are all very serious. I think of the question my family will ask next month at our Passover seder, if we are all still alive by then: *Why is this night different from all other nights?* And

I ask myself, *Why is this drill different from all other drills?* The answer is simple:

Because today may or may not be the end of the world.

My parents were talking about it at breakfast. Somewhere in Pennsylvania, there has been an accident at a nuclear power plant called Three Mile Island. One of the reactors is melting down. I don't understand exactly what that means, but according to my dad, if the reaction isn't stopped, there is going to be a huge radioactive explosion. I guess Three Mile Island is a couple hours south and west of our house, but nobody knows whether we are far enough away to be safe. Besides, my parents say the wind blows from the south and west to the north and east.

That means if the explosion doesn't get us, the huge cloud of radiation will probably blow straight over here. "Nuclear fallout" is what they call it, and apparently, it is a very, very bad thing.

All of a sudden, the drill seems like a really big deal. For once in my life, I do exactly as the teacher says. I skootch my tushy into the wall. I think about my parents. I think about Lissa. I think about Hecky. Does nuclear fallout kill snakes? Or will she mutate into a *super snake*? Because that would be kind of awesome.

Though I guess I wouldn't be around to check it out.

I think about my Aunt Sylvia and my Great-Grandma Rose in Brooklyn. My Aunt Ida in Queens. My Cousin Shira in Manhattan. For the first time in my life, I am happy all my grandparents moved away to Florida when I was little. At least *they* should be safe if that whole Three Mile Island place goes BOOM!

After the drill ends, Miss Tuff reads to us from a science fiction book by an author with a funny name: Andrew J. Offutt. The story is great, and every day when she gets to the end of the chapter, we have all been begging her to read more. But I can't concentrate today. I look around the room. I look at all my new friends and feel sad. I even feel sad when I look at Albert's face, which is still slightly bruised. Sure, he was going to beat me up, and I only saved myself by whacking him in the face with my lunch box. And it's not like he and I have become pals, although I have high hopes that we might be done fighting. Maybe he will speak to me now that the swelling around his nose has mostly gone down.

And anyway, even he doesn't deserve to get blown up at age nine.

Nothing that used to bother me seems important anymore. It all seems so small when there is a nuclear accident hanging over everything. This goes on for days and days, until the guy on my mom's *Eleven O'Clock News* show announces that the crisis is over. But I don't get a break, because right after that, my father goes to see Dr. Suarez about a bump on his forearm. The same forearm he was rubbing after we rode Space Mountain. The same forearm he had to put ice on after the last time we boxed. This must be the appointment my mom was talking about when I was eavesdropping on their big argument!

Dr. Suarez sends him to another doctor, and *that* doctor sends him to *another* nother doctor. Finally, I am up in my closet eavesdropping when my dad says the C word to my mother. The last doctor has stuck a long needle into my dad's arm to take a sample and send it away to a lab. But the doctor has already told my father he is pretty sure what the test will say.

Apparently, my dad has cancer.

I sit there on my shelf in the dark, crying. I know all about cancer. My dad's mom, my Nana Adele, died of it when I was in second grade. First, she started coughing a lot. Then she had a fever all the time. Then she started shrinking and shrinking until she didn't even really look much like the grandmother who had always taken Lissa and me out for ice cream when we used to visit her apartment in New Jersey. The one who always had room for me on her lap. The one who had bought me my favorite Tonka fire truck. The one who had always taken care of me when I was sick.

When I was little, I always thought Nana Adele was a nurse, because she worked in the gigantic Johnson & Johnson factory in New Jersey, and always smelled like Band-Aids. Plus, my very first memory is of a time when I got a high fever, and she stayed up with me all night, wiping my face with a cold washcloth and rubbing my body down with alcohol to lower my temperature. I begged her to just let me sleep, but she never left my side.

Grandmothers who take care of sick people aren't supposed to *become* sick people.

And I remember when the phone call came to say she had died. My father was supposed to fly to Florida to see her the next morning, and while he was down there, he was going to go to my cousin Michael's bar mitzvah. He was all packed up and ready. My parents were standing in the kitchen arguing, because my mother wanted to go with him so she could say goodbye to Nana Adele. My father was saying she could say goodbye on the phone, because we didn't have the money for another ticket, "and besides, the kids are in school. You have to be here to take care of them."

"But, Harv," my mom said, and it was like she was begging. "I love your mother."

"It just doesn't make sense for you to come along right now. And you know *I* wouldn't have gone now if not for my sisters bugging me about it. Plus, there's the bar mitzvah. Otherwise, I would have just waited for the funeral."

My mother's whole face got tight, and I was scared of what she might say. I never found out, because that was when the phone rang. My dad picked it up, listened for a minute, and hung up. Then he turned to my mom and said, "Well, it looks like I won't be missing the funeral after all."

"Oh, *Harv,*" my mother said.

The next morning, after my dad left for the airport, I went outside and stood on our front lawn. It was a beautiful, sunny day, and I thought, *How can it be sunny if my grandmother is dead? It shouldn't be sunny—there should be thunder and lightning! The whole world should be dark.* But the sun just kept beating down. I took out my aluminum baseball bat and a tennis ball from the garage, and made a deal with God: "If I just hit this ball, Nana isn't really dead."

Unfortunately for my grandmother, I am a terrible hitter. I took a tremendous swing but missed the ball completely. Desperately, I picked up the ball from the grass and looked upward at the heavens. "Okay," I said to God. "Two out of three?"

So yeah, I know how this cancer thing works. My grandmother lasted six months, so I count on my fingers: April, May, June, July, August, September.

My father isn't even going to be around for the World Series.

My parents have no idea I know this secret, so when I start getting in trouble in Miss Tuff's class, they don't understand. Everything just kind of falls apart at once. I fall asleep in class, because I haven't been sleeping at night. I tap on my desk even more than usual. I miss steps in class assignments and forget about homework. Worst of all, I start getting into arguments with other kids—not just bullies like Albert, but nice kids. Kids who were starting to feel like new friends.

I snap at everybody. I make fun of people when they get answers wrong in class, or just whenever I think of something mean and funny to say. I can hear the words come out of my mouth, and I feel ashamed, but I can't stop being mean. It's almost like there are two Jordans: the one who says these things, and the one who feels bad about the meanness but can't make it stop. And then, one day, I completely lose my mind. I have been called up to the blackboard to work out a math problem on the board, but the problem is from last night's homework, which I haven't even looked at. I don't know what I am doing, so of course after days of my making fun of everyone who makes a mistake, some kid points it out with a smart comment.

Something breaks open inside me, and I step back a few feet and then hurl an eraser at the board. It makes a tremendous THWAP! sound and sends chalk dust billowing out everywhere. Everybody in the room is staring at me like I am a zoo animal. I run back to my seat and crawl under the desk to hide.

I hear the clacking of Miss Tuff's wooden-heeled sandals on the floor and know she is headed my way. I am in a panic, because Mrs. Fisher slapped me in the face just for missing the Pledge. What is this teacher going to do to me when I have just thrown a fit at the board? I hug my knees, try to slow my breathing, and wait. Miss Tuff kneels down so we are face-to-face. "Oh, honey, I can see that something is really bothering you today. Would you like to come outside with me and talk about what it is?"

Out in the hall, Miss Tuff says, "What is going on with you, Jordan? You can tell me."

I can't look at her. "I am trying so hard to be good, but I *can't* be good! I can't think. I can't listen. How am I supposed to just sit here and do nothing when my dad has . . ." I can't even make myself say the word, but Miss Tuff waits silently until I give it a shot. "C . . . c . . . *cancer*!"

I start to cry so hard that I can't catch my breath. Miss Tuff says, "Oh, I am so sorry! Thank you for being brave enough to tell me. I would hug you, but I know you don't like being touched."

I still can't look at Miss Tuff, but I step forward, throw my arms around her waist, and bury my face in the front of her shirt. When she puts her arms around me, for the first time since September, I feel safe.

17. J.P. Snake

My mother has decided to cheer me up by taking me to the pet shop and buying me a new snake. I don't want another snake. Another snake just means another thing that can die. I have already lost twenty baby snakes and my school this year.

My mom insists, though. "Just come with me to look," she says. "You don't have to buy a snake, but you never know—maybe you'll find one you like."

I think this sounds like a terrible idea, but when my mom throws in a free trip to the comic book store, I stop fighting it. I mean, I really need the next issue of *Marvel Team-Up*, because Spider-Man is going to join forces with the Black Widow—which sounds awesome. Also there's a new *Uncanny X-Men* coming out that looks pretty intriguing. It seems silly to pass up the chance to keep my collection up to date just because I am terrified, depressed, and still in mourning for my slaughtered, innocent garter snakes.

The pet store guy says they have just gotten in a new shipment of garter snakes, and that they seem particularly tame and friendly.

"Feel free to just reach in and pick up whichever one you want to hold," he says.

A very long, unusually fat snake in the back corner of the cage, away from the ten or so others, catches my eye. I am not going to buy this guy, but just holding him couldn't hurt, right?

Except that it does hurt, because the snake strikes without warning and bites my right pointer finger. It's not like I haven't been bitten before, but this snake must have particularly big fangs, because the two punctures on my finger sting and bleed.

Particularly tame? Friendly? I'm thinking the pet store dude isn't too sharp when it comes to reptile psychology. He has a good supply of Band-Aids, antiseptic, and Bacitracin ointment, though.

When I am patched up, I wander back over to the cage. Now I notice a smallish garter snake that has the shiniest, most colorful skin I have ever seen. The black parts of its body are absolutely dark, while the three yellow stripes are almost glow-in-the-dark color. And where the snake's top scales meet its underside, there are striking flecks of red. I am kind of tentative when I reach down this time, but the shiny little guy slithers right over and wraps itself around my wrist.

Like Hecky does!

"Wow, that is a really good-looking snake!" my mother says. "You know, Jord, Hectoria might like having some company." Mom is a great actor, because I happen to know she thinks snakes are revolting. It's nice of her to try, though. And Hecky has been looking a bit mopey lately.

"Whatever," I mumble.

And now I am the owner of two garter snakes.

I am a bit afraid Hecky and this new guy will attack each other, but they don't. I carefully introduce them by draping Hecky over my right hand and the new snake over my left, and slowly bringing the two hands together. They both raise their heads up, and I think, *Oh no! They're going to strike!* They don't strike, though. Instead, Hecky inches forward until her head is just in front of the new snake's, and starts flicking her tongue out again and again. The new snake does the same thing, and I'm pretty sure their tongues actually touch at least once.

Snakes kissing! I am not sure whether I should cheer or barf.

I put the snakes in opposite corners of the cage, just in case. Then I sit down to watch for a while, even though I am dying to read my new comics. Within minutes, Hecky and the new snake have tumbled themselves all over each other. It would be hard to tell which coil belonged to which snake if the new guy weren't so much more vividly colored. Once I am sure nobody is going to eat anybody else, I feel a bit better about this situation, so I leave the snakes alone and head downstairs to the couch to find out how Spidey and the Black Widow get along.

A few days later, I invite Peter Friedman over to meet my

new pet. He insists that we need to give the snake a name. Lying on our backs on my bedroom floor, each of us holding one snake, we brainstorm a million options.

Peter comes up with the Flash, because he moves faster than Hecky does.

I counter with Dash, because of his stripes being so distinctive.

Peter suggests Hector, "because Hecky isn't using it any-more." I shoot that down immediately, because this snake just got here. There's no way I am going to destroy Hecky's self-esteem by suggesting he is equal with her!

I say, "What about Ringo?" Peter says no way, because the snake doesn't have rings, he has stripes.

This goes on for a while. This guy doesn't look like any of the names we come up with. He's not a Blackie or a Stripey (which is way too much like Stripe, anyway) or a Luke Skywalker—which is Peter's extremely dumb suggestion, not mine. Finally, when I am about ready to just beg my mom to drive us back to the mall and return him, I say, "Why don't we name him J.P. Snake?"

"J.P. Snake?" Peter says, turning to squint at me like I have just gone insane. "Why J.P. Snake? Should *Snake* even be in a snake's name? It's not like my name is Peter Friedman Person. And what's the J.P. part for, anyway?"

"That's the genius part: It has two meanings. It could stand for John Paul, like the pope. Or it could be for Jordan Peter. Wouldn't it be cool to have a snake named after us?"

Well, now that this name is in honor of him, Peter loves it. I switch snakes with Peter, who has been holding the new snake the whole time, and hold it so it is looking down at me.

"Welcome to my family," I say to it. "I now pronounce you J.P. Snake."

J.P. Snake celebrates by pooping on my arm a little bit.

Aside from his hygiene issues, J.P. might be good luck, because at the end of the week, my father comes home with amazing news: He doesn't have cancer! The test results have come back from the lab, and it turns out that the weird lump on my dad's arm isn't a deadly weird lump—it's just a regular weird lump. He announces this in the middle of dinner, which

is kind of strange, because Lissa and I aren't even supposed to know about the whole cancer thing, and I don't think my parents have discovered the heating-duct listening trick. But the announcement isn't as strange as my mom's reaction. She starts crying, right there at the table!

I don't get it. Why would she cry because her husband *doesn't* have cancer? This reminds me of the whole fiasco at Hanukkah, when my mom told us not to get her anything and then threw a fit when we listened. If all wives are this confusing, I am never getting married.

Later that night, when I am in bed and the lights are out, I realize I am kind of *mad* at my father. I mean, I am glad he isn't dying. But now I have to go to school and tell Miss Tuff the whole thing was a mistake, and that I was terribly behaved all week for nothing. Then I have to go back to being *good* and *nice* all day again. Which isn't as easy as it sounds.

Just before I fall asleep I figure something out. I guess maybe if I can be angry at my dad for not being sick, it wasn't that weird for my mom to cry when she heard the news.

18. The Ron Hunt of Snug Harbor Little League

Baseball! I love everything about it. I love the yearly ritual of oiling up my glove for the season with my dad. I love meeting my teammates. I love the smell of the fresh-cut grass on the field. I love warming up in the outfield by catching fly balls. I love base-running drills. I love hitting drills. I love trying out for my favorite positions: pitcher and second base.

The best thing about baseball is that every season starts with fresh, new hope.

But the hope never lasts long. I always squirt too much oil on my glove, and then it has weird dark stains that never fade. My teammates always start out liking me, but then they see me in action. It's terrible! I am deathly allergic to grass, so as soon as we hit the field, my eyes water nonstop and I can't breathe. I am so spectacularly awful at catching fly balls that last year, a kid on my team said they should just send my glove out to right field and leave me in the dugout, because the glove might have a better chance of making a play without me around. I am not the fastest base runner in the world and I rarely hit the ball. The saddest part of all of this is that I am great at pitching and playing second base in practice. But when a game comes around, I choke.

Basically, my season has two parts: the Glorious First Two Weeks of Practice, followed by the Horrible Three Months of Sitting on the Bench. The rules of Snug Harbor Little League say that every player has to play at least three innings of each game. So really, I spend only *half* of each game on the bench. But wow, it feels like a lot more.

I have a couple of useful skills, though. I am excellent at cheering for my team super loudly, and at heckling the other team from the dugout until an umpire yells at me to stop. I am good at calming down my teammates when they have messed up on the field. And I am truly gifted when it comes to the fine art of getting hit by the pitch.

And yes, it is an art.

First, you have to crowd the plate, which means standing as close as possible to the strike zone and then leaning over so your upper body is practically *in* the zone. Second, you have to stick out your front elbow as far as it can reach. Third—and most critical—you must *never flinch*. It sounds simple to just stand there and take the hit, but it is not. Your body wants to get out of the way, because baseballs are HARD. Until you have taken one in the ribs, or suffered a direct hit to the funny bone, you can't really appreciate just *how* hard they are.

And a direct hit to the helmet? That will leave you shaky for days—trust me.

But it's all worth it when you get on first base. Then you can taunt and distract the pitcher by taking a lead and dancing just in the corner of his field of vision. It's great, because he is probably already shaken up from hitting you. If you get him thinking you might take off and steal second base, he'll get even more worried. Sometimes this means he will walk or hit the next batter. Sometimes it means he will fall behind in the count and have to throw a ball straight down the middle, where the batter can smack it over the infielders' heads and into the outfield. And sometimes, he'll get so distracted that he misses the catcher completely and you can steal second without even having to slide.

I'm not fast, but I'm smart, which means stealing bases is the second-best part of my game. As long as I don't get knocked out while performing the best part of my game, I have a great shot at getting to second, and maybe even to third. Then if there's a big hit, I can score a run for my team.

Not bad for a kid who can barely see the ball.

My father comes to every single game. He never criticizes my playing, and if I get on base and steal second, he pats me on the shoulder after the game and says, "Great base running, son!" I would love to make a heroic, game-winning play so he could get to say, "Great diving catch, bud!" or "Great hitting, pal!" But I'll take what I can get.

This year, my mom asked specially for me to be put on a team with Peter Friedman. This is great for the parents and their carpooling needs, and I admit I love having Peter around. It is *not* great for my playing, though. Pete is a year older than me, so I am the youngest kid on the opening-day roster for our team, Lockwood Plumbing. I am short for my own age, but when you put me on a field with a bunch of fifth graders, it looks like somebody on the team is a ventriloquist and I am his dummy.

Leaving me out of the picture for a minute, I have to say our team has some great players. We have two unbelievable pitchers, Nick and Tommy. Tommy never walks anybody, which my dad says is nearly 100 percent of how you win in Little League. He also has a weird, floaty, curveball-type pitch that makes kids take huge swings and miss the ball completely. Sometimes, they even fall down! But the real star is Nick. He never walks anybody, either—plus, he throws the ball about a million miles an hour. I have batted against him in practice, and it is terrifying. When my bad eyesight combines with his pitch speed, I might as well just wear a blindfold and attempt to hit the ball using only my sense of smell.

But since he's on my team, at least I don't have to face his deadly fireballs in a real game.

We also have maybe five really good hitters and a big, mean catcher named Garrett, who terrifies opposing players when he blocks home plate. Then there are guys like Peter, who are decent, but sometimes get benched. The last three kids, the ones who live on the bench, are me, a huge kid named Garth who is bigger than our coach but not very coordinated, and a boy named Scott who wears big metal braces around his lower legs.

Garth, Scott, and I spend a lot of time together since we

are always sitting out. The good news is that those guys are nice. That makes me feel extra bad when Scott comes up to bat and his dad yells at him. It's awful! Here's a kid who can barely walk, and his own father screams at him, "Hit the ball! What's wrong with you? Don't you even want to win?"

I hope one day Scott hits a line drive straight into the stands and nails his dad right on the head.

The problem is even worse when Scott is in the outfield. If Scott makes an error, his father screams, "What are you, afraid of the ball?" This is the worst thing anybody can say to a kid. Being slow, being clumsy, even making a stupid mental mistake—all of these things aren't unforgivably embarrassing. But being Afraid of the Ball is different. If you are Afraid of the Ball, everyone thinks less of you. They think you are a wimp. They think you are not a *man*.

I make a lot of errors in the field, too, and I have always been terrified that somebody might say I am Afraid of the Ball. I think they probably would, too, except for my excellent track record of getting hit by the pitch. Anybody who Takes One for the Team on a regular basis can't be Afraid of the Ball. Taking One for the Team is the exact opposite of being Afraid of the Ball. In fact, when a kid gets hit by the pitch and then jogs down to first base, our coach, Mr. Dave, always slaps him on the shoulder and says, "Way to take it like a man!"

Sure, it hurts getting smashed in the kidney by a fastball. But I would rather lose a kidney than my *reputation*.

Choices like this come up a lot in my life, for some reason.

In fact, just after the beginning of the baseball season, Peter Friedman and I get into a fight with three fifth graders at school. I have been trying super-duper-extra hard to be good since the end of my dad's battle with fake cancer, but there is no way to avoid this trouble. Pete is pretty big, but there's a kid in his grade named Darren who is at least his size. Also, Darren is super obnoxious. Pete has a serious skin rash on his face right now. There is an angry ring of red completely surrounding his lips, and some kids have started teasing him about it. One day in the hall, Darren starts calling Pete "Ronald McDonald." Pete pushes him, Darren pushes back, and the only thing that stops them from going at it right then and there is that our assistant principal, Mr. Levy, comes around the corner at just that moment.

But the fight is going to happen. It's just a matter of time.

Just like Albert when he tried to bully me, Darren goes everywhere with two smaller fifth graders at his sides. They laugh and say, "Yeah!" whenever he unleashes one of his stupid insults. Anyway, Peter and I meet at the end of the school day to walk outside and wait for his mom, who is almost always late, to pick us up for Little League practice. As soon as we step out the front door of the school, Darren and his two mini-Darrens step in front of us so we can't get down the front steps.

I am really hoping we won't have to fight, or at least that we won't have to fight ON THE FRONT STEPS OF THE SCHOOL, but Darren unleashes his "Ronald McDonald" line again. I try to step between them and hold Pete back, but that becomes pointless when Darren does the one thing no boy can ignore without ruining his reputation forever. He face-chumps Peter.

Here's what a face-chump is: You press the edge of your hand against the front of somebody's forehead. Then you push the other person's forehead hard while saying, "Face chump! THANK YOU!"

Here's what a face-chump does: It starts a fight. There is simply no way around it. If you get face-chumped and don't immediately either hit or tackle the kid who did it, you are a wimp. Ignoring a face-chump might even be worse than being Afraid of the Ball, because if you dodge a baseball, nobody throws a bunch of additional baseballs at you. But if you just walk away after a face-chump, *lots* of people are going to throw a bunch of additional face-chumps your way.

To make it even worse, Pete is wearing his favorite New York Yankees cap, which he got for his last birthday when we went to Yankee Stadium. Darren's face-chump makes Pete's hat fly off his head, over the railing at the side of the school's front porch, and onto a bush.

Nobody knocks my friend's beloved Yankees cap into a bush. I turn away from Peter and shove Darren with all my might. His back smashes into the wall, and his sidekicks step forward between us. For a second, each of us just stares his enemies down. Then Darren pushes off the wall, just as Peter yells, "You take the two little ones! I got the big one!"

It's on.

Pete pushes his way between the two smaller guys and tackles Darren around the waist. I grab the closest smaller guy—who is still a bit bigger than my tiny fourth-grade self—and shove him against the fence rail. The other one snatches *my* authentic, Major League Baseball–certified Yankees cap off my head and holds it over the edge of the porch like he's going to drop it. I reach for the hat, and my elbow connects with his chin, hard.

He drops my hat onto the bush.

I hope the bush is a Yankee fan.

The next thing I know, I am wrestling with two fifth graders at once. I hear Peter and Darren shouting at each other, but I

can't look to see what is happening on the ground, because I am concentrating on turning around and around as fast as I can so my opponents can't get a good grip on me.

Then, just as my glasses go flying off my face and into the bush, which is getting very crowded with our possessions, I remember my father's helpful fighting tips. He never coached me about how to box two people at once, but still, I figure I shouldn't let my opponent take the first shot. It's time for a maneuver Peter and I have only ever practiced in his basement: *Throwing a Hulk.* It's a simple strategy: You go completely nuts and attack absolutely *everything.* I figure it is a particularly smart move now that I can't see who I'm fighting.

I'm surrounded, so I can't miss.

Throwing a Hulk turns out to be both effective and *extremely* satisfying. I swing my fists wildly in every direction, and hear several cries of "Ow!" along with one "This kid is a maniac!"

That's right, chumps. I'm a *maniac*!

I don't know how long this goes on, but eventually, I end up rolling around on the concrete with both my enemies on top of me. Still swinging like a madman, I am snapped out of my rage when Peter shouts, "Run!" Not surprisingly, considering we are still on the school porch, Mr. Levy has noticed the commotion and is shouting at us from the bus lines through a bullhorn. Lucky for us the bus stops are a couple of hundred feet away. One of the kids I have just been punching helps me up, and we all grab our backpacks and make a break for it. As a group, we push our way through all the walkers crossing the street and the kids in the car lines, and—somehow—we make it around the far corner of the school without any grown-ups grabbing us.

A very blurry Peter and a very blurry Darren peek back around the corner and then burst out laughing.

"Levy went the wrong way!" Darren gasps. "He's crossing the street!"

"Awesome," Peter wheezes.

"Yeah, but I still have to go back and get my glasses," I moan. "Then there's no *way* we won't be busted."

"Stay here," one of my opponents says. I can't tell which one, because I can't see, and even if I could see, I don't know either of their names anyway. Before anybody can say anything else, he strolls back toward the front of the school. The rest of us wait nervously for a couple of minutes, and then the kid is back. He presses my glasses into my hand, and I slip them on. They're a bit bent, but they've been worse.

Then he casually tosses me and Pete our baseball caps.

"Thanks," we both say, and the Battle of the Front Steps is officially over. The three other fifth graders walk away, leaving me and Pete standing by ourselves.

"Nice one," Pete says, smiling.

"You too. You were totally winning," I say. "Those guys are lucky Levy showed up and saved their lives." We walk back to the front sidewalk, where Pete's mom has just pulled up to the curb, and climb into her car without another word.

19. Welcome to Pennsylvania: The Overwhelming State

When Miss Tuff tells us we have one more major assignment for the year, and that it is an encyclopedia report on one of the fifty states, I get excited. I know how to write an encyclopedia report! I've done the *Merrimack* and the *Monitor*, the Komodo dragon, the *Tyrannosaurus rex*—how different can this be?

The answer is: SUPER different! I pick Pennsylvania, because I love going to summer camp there. Miss Tuff hands me the *P* volume of the *World Book Encyclopedia*, and it's not the same *World Book* I know from my first-grade experiences. That was the young readers' encyclopedia. I guess this is the old readers' version, and it is huge. Plus, the print is about half as big as what I am used to. The pictures are much smaller. And the entry on Pennsylvania is twenty-two pages long!

From what I have seen of Pennsylvania, I can't believe anybody could find twenty-two pages' worth of stuff to write about the place. I kind of figured there would be three pages:

one about the Liberty Bell and the movie *Rocky*, one about Three Mile Island, and one about the woods. But there is an unbelievable amount of information in this thing. The history of the state is eleven pages. Then there is a huge section on the state's geography, another one on tourism, and one about the economy—whatever *that* is.

And there is absolutely nothing about Three Mile Island, which means I won't have an excuse to draw an awesome atomic explosion for my cover.

We have about forty-five minutes each day for two weeks to work on this project. I spend the first two days just reading the Pennsylvania pages—and getting shushed by Camille Adinolfi and Stephanie Casella because I tap my pencil on things when I read. I spend the third day working on a cover design, because a report is doomed if it doesn't have a good cover. I try to draw the Liberty Bell three times, but I just can't get it right. I actually think the third one is okay if you squint hard, but when I show it to Camille and ask her what she thinks it is, she says, "A telephone! That's really good! Did Alexander Graham Bell live in Pennsylvania? I thought he lived in New Jersey. Wow, I am learning a lot from this project already!"

To be fair, the Liberty Bell does look a lot like a telephone. I try to draw a crack in the bell so the difference is clear, but then it just looks like a *broken* telephone. I crumple up the Liberty Phone and spike it into the trash can with all my might.

Miss Tuff has been talking a lot about being thorough

and neat. She has also said we should outline our projects before we start writing, so I spend the fourth day making a fancy-looking outline in my best cursive, with a different colored marker for each section. Unfortunately, it turns out that the yellow ink in the marker I have used for the "economy" section is completely invisible, which sends me back to the garbage can.

This project has to be *perfect* so Miss Tuff is proud of me.

When I look around the room on day five, I can't help but notice that B.J.'s project on New Hampshire already makes an impressive pile of pages on his desk. I don't know how he could possibly be finding so much to write about such a small state, but then again, his family spends a week there every summer on vacation, so maybe he is writing about that.

At lunch on the sixth day, B.J. announces that he's finished.

"With the whole project?" I ask.

He nods.

"Even the cover?"

He nods again.

"Even the *economy* section?"

He smiles modestly and says, "Well, New Hampshire doesn't have much of an economy."

Other kids at our table laugh. I bet I would, too, except I still don't understand what an economy *is*. It can't be the same as a capital, because I have already learned that the capital of Pennsylvania is Harrisburg, but the economy section barely mentions Harrisburg at all. It's just a bunch of numbers and stuff about steel and coal. But hey! That gives me a foolproof idea for the cover!

When we get back up to our classroom, I spend the next forty-five minutes drawing a pile of coal and a cube made out of steel girders. A few minutes before we are going to run out of time, I feel like my cover is missing some extra touch of genius to make it perfect, so I draw some wavy lines above the coal to show it is on fire.

When I am done, I hold the paper at arm's length to see how it looks.

I am pretty sure it is a masterpiece.

A few minutes later, Miss Tuff changes my seat because Camille says I threw a paper ball at her. Miss Tuff doesn't even care that I have an excellent reason. Camille. She looked at my report cover and asked me why I was drawing a steaming pile of poop.

Now I have wasted another day, and I still don't have a cover. Or a report. All I have is an outline, although I have to admit it is a very *colorful* outline.

On day seven, Miss Tuff dismisses everybody who is done with the report to go outside for recess, and announces she is going to come around and check in with the rest of us about our progress. What am I supposed to say? "I'm making excellent progress in filling up the garbage can"? "I now know that an *economy* and a *Harrisburg* are two different things"? "I accidentally learned how to draw a pile of poop"?

I panic and ask to go see the nurse.

By the time I get back, I have missed half of the day's read-aloud. Now not only do I have no report with three days to go, I am also completely lost in Andrew Offutt's story. I don't even know which aliens are the good-guy aliens and which ones are trying to destroy the universe. That makes it impossible to pay attention. My mind wanders, and I start thinking about how I am a lot like a space alien. Really, I am a good guy, but everybody else *thinks* I am trying to ruin things. The problem is, how can you tell a good-guy alien from a bad-guy alien?

Maybe I should wear a T-shirt that says I'M NICE in huge letters across the front. But then again, that is exactly what a *bad-guy alien* would probably do.

I suppose all I can do is keep trying to be good. There is always a chance it will work eventually.

On the eighth day, I decide I really need to start writing. I crank out three pages, front and back. This is the most I have ever written in one day. My pencil callus is not up to the challenge, which means I have a huge blister on the side of my pointer finger by the end. Also, the entire pinkie side of my hand is coated with pencil dust, because I hold my pencil wrong and drag my hand across the page.

I blame Miss Williamsen. If she had done a better job teaching penmanship in second grade, I would probably have a lot more of this report done by now—and my hand would be spotless. I bet these things never happen to William Feranek.

Of course, he is still back at P.S. 35, where all the encyclopedias are simple to use. I almost wish I had stayed there, except for the fact that Mrs. Fisher would probably have set me on fire or something by now. While Britt Stone toasted marshmallows.

Miss Tuff must have noticed how much writing I got done, because on our way to art class, she says, "I saw how hard you were working today, Jordan. You must have gotten a lot done. I'm proud of you!"

I blush. I *did* get a lot done today, but I'm not even halfway done with the history section. Even if I write again at top speed tomorrow, the best I can hope for is that I will finish up that part. Then I will only have one day left to do geography, tourism, and economy, plus the cover.

By the end of art class, I have made a very heroic decision. "Miss Tuff," I ask, "may I borrow the *P* encyclopedia tonight to work on my project?"

She grins at me. "Well, I don't usually allow students to take encyclopedia volumes home, but for you, I can make an exception. I know I can trust you to take care of it."

I place the book in my backpack super carefully. Miss Tuff is right. She can trust me. I would dive in front of a radioactive materials truck for Miss Tuff in a heartbeat. If I can do that, how hard can it be to protect one simple book?

A few hours later, I am sitting at the dining room table of my house, surrounded by several sheets of construction paper, a pile of loose-leaf pages, a box of colored pencils, the encyclopedia, and a glass of orange juice. I have written eight pages, the blisters on my hand are now actually oozing fluid, and I am still not even done with the history section.

I am trying to make my writing shorter than what's in the book, but it is very hard. For example, there is a sentence in the encyclopedia that goes, *In 1614, Cornelius Jacobsen Mey became the first known European to reach Pennsylvania when he entered Delaware Bay in the employ of Dutch merchants interested in the fur trade.* I change this around to, *Cornelius Jacobsen Mey was probably the first European to enter PA. In 1614, he came to Delaware Bay looking for furs. He was known.* This is basically as long as the original, even though I left out the part about Dutch merchants.

Also, I'm pretty sure it doesn't make sense.

My mom asks me to clear the table so she can get ready to serve dinner, and I say, "I can't! I have to work!"

When I explain the problem to her, she says, "Jord, if you try to write down *everything*, you'll never get done. You just need to include the important things."

I slam my orange juice glass down on the table and shout, "BUT IT'S *ALL* IMPORTANT!" This makes my mom jump. It also makes the juice jump—straight up out of the glass and onto the cover of the encyclopedia. I burst out crying. Now Miss Tuff will never trust me again!

My mom runs into the kitchen, grabs a handful of paper towels, and blots the OJ off the book. "Oh, honey, it's okay. Look, the juice came right off! See? You can stop crying. We will work this out." She sits down next to me and starts reading what I have written. "You don't need to write all of this. If you just jot down a few major events for each page, and then retell them in your own words, you can get the whole paper done much faster."

My mother doesn't understand. I can't just "jot down" a few things. That is probably what everybody else is doing. My project has to be long, neat, detailed, and *perfect*. I push my stuff aside long enough to choke down the smallest possible amount of food I can get away with eating, and then as soon as the dishes are cleared, I get right back to work: *In 1638, the Swedes, under Governor Johan Printz, began to settle and farm the fertile banks of the Delaware River, eventually causing friction with the Dutch government. Also, there were forts.*

I barely make it to school on the ninth day. My pointer finger is sporting a new Band-Aid, there are gigantic purple bags under my eyes from lack of sleep, and I am pretty sure the encyclopedia still smells like a citrus fruit. But I have conquered the history section. Now it is on to geography!

This time, when Miss Tuff sends the kids who are done out to play, I am one of only three students left inside. She comes over to my desk and stands over me as I start writing. I can feel beads of sweat breaking out all over my body. What if she hates my work? What if I get in trouble for not working fast enough? *What if she can smell the juice?*

"Jordan," she says, sitting down in the empty seat next to me, "can I show you something?"

I nod, terrified. Now her nose is even closer to the book!

"I am very proud of you for all the hard work you have been doing, but I think you can make life a lot simpler for yourself if you do things a bit differently. What you are doing is called *paraphrasing*. That's when you switch around some of the words in each sentence from your source but still keep in nearly everything from the original. You don't need to paraphrase every sentence. In fact, you *shouldn't* paraphrase every sentence. Paraphrasing is a form of copying."

"But . . ." I whine, trying not to let her hear the shakiness of my voice. "I'm trying to make my report thorough. You *said* we had to be thorough. I'm not trying to copy. I am trying to be *good*."

Miss Tuff puts her hand gently on my shoulder. "Oh, Jordan, what am I going to do with you? You *are* good. I see it every day."

I look at her in disbelief. "I'm *not* good every day."

"Your behavior might not always be perfect. But you are a good person. Now, here's what we are going to do . . ."

She tells me to stop what I am doing, jot down a few major events for each page of the encyclopedia entry, and then just write a paragraph in my own words to describe each event. I can't believe it! My mother was right, and I could have saved hours and hours of work.

Stupid jotting down.

I ask Miss Tuff if I can have the weekend to finish my project, even though that means it will be a day late. She says, "Of course. I think it is great that you are so conscientious."

Wow, I am conscientious! I can't wait to look that word up so I can find out what it means. But before I do that, I have one last question: "Miss Tuff, do I have to go back and redo everything I have already written?"

When she says no, I feel like crying again. Just then, the other kids come back in from recess. Miss Tuff rubs my hair and walks away. As I place the encyclopedia in my backpack, I realize something: I haven't pulled my hair at all for weeks! I haven't even thought about pulling it.

I feel pretty sad about this stupid project, but I also kind of want to smile, because Miss Tuff thinks I am *conscientious*. I sit up and puff my chest out a bit—like the ruffed grouse, Pennsylvania's state bird. Maybe this is what it is like to be kind of happy.

20. Stubby and Skip

My parents are fighting. It starts when my mom's Chevy Nova breaks down on the way to Rutgers. The car is really old, and the mechanics at Sam & Nick's on Forest Avenue say she should buy a new one. My parents decide she should get a hatchback so it has room for a lot of stuff if we go on long trips. Mom wants either a VW Rabbit like her best friend, Judy Friedman, has or a Honda Civic like the one her boss, Lou, drives. Mom says those cars are more reliable than American ones, and they get better gas mileage. Dad says that our family buys American cars. Also, the Rabbit and the Civic are both stick-shift cars, and he points out that she doesn't know how to drive a stick shift. He tells her she needs to buy a Chevy Citation, which is a totally new hatchback model.

I don't care what she buys, as long as she doesn't get stuck on the highway in New Jersey again. That's how the mom of one of those kids I knew died. She was pulled over on the shoulder of the road and got hit by a car while she was waiting in the dark for a tow truck.

Mom takes Lissa and me out for two test drives of the stick-shift cars. When she is driving Judy's car, it stalls about a million times. Also, when we are moving, the car keeps jerking and feels like it is about to explode. The same thing happens when she takes Lou's car out for a spin. Lissa and I make each other laugh the whole time by making throw-up faces in the back seat, but it really does feel like we are going to get thrown out through the roof any second. At one point, she tries to park on a steep hill near her office by the Staten Island Ferry, and the car starts rolling backward. Lou has to grab the emergency brake lever and yank up on it to keep us from zooming into an intersection.

Judy and Lou both say my mom will be a stick-shift master if she just practices a few more times. Dad says there's no point, because she is buying a Citation. I can see Dad's point about the stick-shift issue. On the other hand, Mom is right that her Nova, and my dad's even older bright orange one, breaks down a lot. And they are both Chevys. It would be very comforting to know she was in a car that would make it all the way to Rutgers and all the way home every single time.

Between the arguments and the constant thought that my mother's car doesn't work right, I start pulling my hair out again. It gets so bad that my mom notices. We have a long talk about it one night when she gets home super late, comes in to say good night, and finds hairs all over my pillow. Well, we don't exactly have a talk. It's more of a cry.

Mom tells me she is safe and I don't have to worry about her.

Then she makes me promise I won't pull my hair out anymore. I make the promise, but we are both lying. She is not safe, and the very next time she has class, she comes home twenty minutes late. I try not to pull, but as the minutes tick away, I panic and can't help myself. When she gets home, I run to the door and say, "I'm sorry! I'm sorry! I *pulled* again!" Mom starts to weep.

Good, I think. *Maybe now she'll drop out of graduate school and stay safe.*

I'm not sure whether my dad knows about the pulling, because he is not very observant. I think he probably wouldn't notice anything was different about my hair unless it was actively on fire in the middle of dinner. Which is pretty improbable, because he is almost never home for dinner.

But whether he knows about my hair problem or not, my father starts bringing up the possibility of her quitting grad school again. He says, "You wouldn't even need a new car if you didn't put so much extra mileage on it going back and forth to New Jersey!" Half of me is cheering for him, but I am shocked to find that the other half of me agrees with what she says next: "Harv, I've come this far. I *have* to finish now, or it will all have been for nothing." I kind of do want her to get the doctoral degree after all this. I have sacrificed my hair for this degree! If I had to be miserable all this time, and my mom doesn't even get a diploma at the end, I will be even more disgusted than I already am.

I also realize that what I think doesn't matter, because as soon as my father even raises the slightest possibility of her quitting, I know my mom will never, ever do it. All that happens is that she gets more determined, which makes them fight more, which makes her even *more* determined. I feel like I am trapped in the back of a lurching VW Rabbit, with no end in sight.

The fighting doesn't exactly stop. It just sort of dies down as each of my parents gets something they want. Mom keeps going to school, and Dad makes her buy a Citation. So everybody is miserable, but we have a shiny new vehicle. At least my mother knows how to drive this one.

For a week, I sleep well. Then the new car breaks down on the New Jersey Turnpike.

I have always loved drawing little cartoons, especially during class. I have a whole section at the back of my loose-leaf binder full of page after page of spaceship battles, X-Men fight scenes, illustrated jokes, and funny comic strips. One day, Miss Tuff catches me drawing an episode of my newest creation, *Stubby the Triple Amputee and His Two-Legged Dog, Skip*. The joke behind every Stubby and Skip cartoon is that instead of regular artificial hands, feet, or paws, Stubby and Skip both have curved hooks at the end of each cut-off limb, Captain Hook–style. Anyway, I am very absorbed in the fine details of *Stubby and Skip Go Fishing*, drawing bait worms impaled on each of the characters' hooks, which are stuck in the water over the side of a rowboat. I don't notice my teacher standing over my shoulder until she asks, "What are you drawing there?"

I tell her the whole Stubby and Skip story, and frankly, I am quite surprised when she doesn't laugh. All she says is "Very interesting." Then she asks me whether she can borrow my art for a while.

Later that day, I hear my name over the intercom. I am being called down to the office, with my things! This is terrible! All the kids go, *"Oooooooooh!"* and stare. Then there is the long, terrifying walk down the stairs and up the hallway, which gives me plenty of time to worry about what I have done wrong.

I can't think of *anything*.

A big, tall guy with glasses, a bald spot, and a gigantic belly is waiting for me at the office door. This is weird—he isn't Mr. Levy or the principal, Mr. Savitz. I can feel the panic rising in my throat. I haven't been called down to see the assistant principal. I haven't been called down to see the principal. *What's even more powerful than a principal?* I wonder. *Is this guy the super-principal? The principal of principals? What if this man is the legendary New York City chancellor of public schools, Dr. Frank J. Macchiarola?*

Whatever I have done, it must be something even worse than the Great Crayon Melting of '78.

The man introduces himself as Mr. Greenberg, shakes my hand, and leads me into a small side room with no windows. It looks like the kind of place where the cops go when they want to interrogate a prisoner. I don't know who this Greenberg character is, but as he takes a seat facing me from just a couple of feet away, I vow he isn't going to break my will.

"Jordan," he says, "you're probably wondering why I've called you down today."

I say, "Um, I guess so." But really, I am thinking, *No duh!*

"It's about your artwork. I am your school guidance counselor. Do you know what that means?"

I kind of have a vague idea. "Uh, you talk to kids?"

He laughs and then says, "That's about it. I talk to kids when they are sad or worried or mad. Can you tell me about this picture you drew in class?" He takes *Stubby and Skip Go Fishing* out of a drawer in his desk.

One edge of the picture has gotten creased. Grr.

I take a deep breath, force a smile onto my face, and tell Mr. Greenberg all about Stubby and Skip. I am in the middle of explaining why fishing with foot-hooks is funny when he cuts me off.

"Jordan," he says, "do you think maybe you might be angry about something? Because this picture seems kind of angry to me."

This is weird. I didn't make this cartoon because I was mad. I made it because I thought it would be funny. It's a good thing he doesn't know about the story I wrote in Mrs. Dowd's third-grade class. It was called "Love Luck," and it was about a series of people who murder each other while out on dates.

Mrs. Dowd never said anything about the story. She just stamped GOOD on top of my paper in red.

Anyway, I don't *think* I'm mad. I'm scared my mother is going to die. I'm worried that everyone in the world will decide I am nuts because I can't seem to stop pulling the hair out of my head. I don't like it that my parents have been fighting more than usual. I wasn't thrilled when Mrs. Fisher whacked me across the face. And, I mean, there were those two fights I've gotten into in my first six weeks at P.S. 54, but I didn't get into them because I was mad. I got into them because bigger kids wanted to hurt me. You'd smash a kid in the face with a lunch box if he wouldn't let you walk to your mom's car in peace, too. Wouldn't you?

Wouldn't you?

Okay, maybe I am a little irritated. But I tell him, "No, I'm not mad. I was just making a joke."

"Are you sure?" he asks.

I swallow. "Yes, I'm sure."

Just then, the phone on the desk rings. I jump. When Mr. Greenberg picks up, I can hear the secretary say, "Jordan Sonnenblick's mother is here."

They called my mom? I think. *Now I'm mad!*

But I don't think this goes the way Mr. Greenberg had expected. He gives a whole speech about how the "school intervention team" is concerned about me, how I might be working out anger issues through my "disturbing" art, blah blah blah. Then he shows my mother the cartoon.

She reads it and cracks up. That pretty much kills the meeting.

164

The next day in class, everybody wants to know why I got called down to the office and what happened. I don't reveal anything. Stephanie Casella puts her hand on my shoulder in the hallway and says, "Was it really bad?"

I nod solemnly. "It was awful," I say.

It's kind of fun being The Kid Who Got In Big Trouble. I should be mad at Miss Tuff for turning my cartoon over to the big dude downstairs, but I am kind of grateful that she didn't just yell at me in class and rip it up like Mrs. Fisher would have. Instead, she tried to get help for me, which means she really does care.

And hey, I enjoy being a famous outlaw for a while.

21. Magic and Work

I hate my left hand. It is a useless lump. My right hand likes playing drums. It cooperates with my brain. When I tell my right hand to hit a drum during a lesson, or the dictionary at home, it obeys. And if I tell my right hand to hit the dictionary twice in a row, it can do that for me, too.

But the left hand sometimes hits the drum twice when I want it to hit only once. Or it hits three times when I am trying to play a double stroke roll, and then I am like, *Stupid hand. Why do you think they call it a double stroke roll? Does the word double have any meaning for you at all?* It is quite frustrating having an idiot attached to one of my arms.

The difference between my right hand and my left has gotten more and more noticeable as the weeks and months have gone on and Mr. Stoll has made my practice assignments harder. He does this by using the metronome, which has turned out to be a tool of evil. The way it works is that you set the speed of the clicks using the knob on top, and then that becomes the beat you're supposed to play along with when you practice. Whenever I get the hang of a rudiment or a reading exercise, Mr. Stoll figures out how fast I've been playing it and sets the metronome five or ten beats per minute faster for the next week.

Usually my right hand is totally fine with the new speed, but my left hand starts flapping around like it's been set on fire.

So this one week, when I can't get an exercise in *Stick Control for the Snare Drummer* up to the right speed, I just give up and quit practicing. Not only that, but I decide that I might as well skip the new page I am supposed to learn in *Rolls, Rolls, Rolls*. I feel like a percussion delinquent. The next thing you know, I'll be smoking cigarettes and then putting them out against the cover of my dictionary.

I still practice the easier things, like my latest Jedi assignment: the long roll. A long roll is just a double stroke roll that you start very slowly and then gradually speed up until you are playing as fast as you can without messing up the right-right-left-left pattern. Mr. Stoll says eventually I will be able to get as fast as he is, but I don't know. By the end of Mr. Stoll's long roll, the tips of the sticks are too fast for my eyes to follow, and the noise doesn't sound like the sticks are individually hitting the drum. All my ears can hear is a smooth zipping buzz, kind of like somebody is tearing a very long piece of paper. I don't mind working on this rudiment, though, because after a while, I don't even have to think about it. My wrists just know what to do.

The other thing I absolutely don't stop doing is listening to the Beatles album and hitting my dictionary on the beat. As long as I do this with only my right hand, I feel like I am becoming an expert at keeping time. At my lessons, Mr. Stoll gives me a chance to sit at the set and keep time on each of the different kinds of cymbals. He tells me that the more relaxed I am while I do this, the more I become a true timekeeper.

A true timekeeper. Nothing in the world could possibly be more heroic than that. Someday, when I die, I hope my widow gets it carved on my tombstone.

HERE LIES JORDAN SONNENBLICK

A HUSBAND

A FATHER

A TRUE TIMEKEEPER

If only the pathetic left hand would get with the program, I'd probably be a true timekeeper by now. But if I relax that sad hunk of meat for even a second, I am likely to lose my grip, sending a drumstick flying across the room. Mr. Stoll says everybody naturally has a dominant hand and a weaker hand, and that the more I practice, the more equal my hands will become. But I have already been doing this for months, and the left idiot is not exactly jumping on the equality train.

Once I start letting my practice routine slide, it gets easier and easier to skip everything in my drum books. Soon, you can practically see a layer of dust forming on top of *Stick Control*.

Finally, Mr. Stoll notices. I start to play the week's assigned page in *Rolls, Rolls, Rolls*, which I haven't even looked at. He can tell right away that I am trying to read the notes for the first time, so he cuts me off. His blue eyes, which are usually super mild and friendly, bore into me as he asks, "So, Jordan, how many times have you gone over this page?"

I look down at my lap.

"Haven't you practiced it at all?"

If I had heat vision, my lap would be in flames by now.

Mr. Stoll sighs. "Jordan," he says, "your mother asked me whether I think you're ready for a snare drum of your own. I told her I thought so, because you've been working hard. But if you don't keep practicing, then you won't really be *earning* the drum. Besides, I don't feel right taking your parents' money if you don't want to put the time in."

I feel terrible. Mr. Stoll hasn't raised his voice or anything, but I would almost feel better if he had. This is awful! He has trusted me with the best album in the whole world. He has been totally patient with me and my failure of a left hand. *He has told my mom I deserve a snare drum*. And I have thrown it all away.

I picture myself sitting in the cold waters of Fairview Lake with Louise Boily. I know what she would say, and she would be right. I am not zee kind of boy who lets go of zee rope. Getting up on skis looked like a magic trick, but really it was just about hanging on. Maybe drumming is like that, too. Maybe even though it looks like magic, it's really *work*.

"I'm sorry, Mr. Stoll," I say to my lap. Then I force myself to look my teacher in the face. "I *do* want to put the time in."

"Okay," he says. "From the top. *Slowly*."

22. Bottom of the Order

I am starting to think our coach, Mr. Dave, isn't a very good strategist. In every game, he puts Garth, Scott, and me all in a row in the batting order, hitting seventh, eighth, and ninth. This is a terrible idea, because we are almost guaranteed to make three outs in a row—which is kind of a rally killer. Also, batting all in a row makes it even more obvious to the rest of the team, and the parents in the stands, that the three of us are awful.

One game in May is the absolute worst. Going into the bottom of the last inning, Lockwood Plumbing is down by one run. The fourth, fifth, and sixth hitters all get on base with no outs. This brings Garth up to the plate. Everybody is screaming and yelling. Our whole team is hanging off the mesh fence that protects the dugout, shouting our favorite team chant at the top of our lungs: "We want a pitcher! Not a belly itcher!"

Which totally doesn't make sense, but whatever. The pitcher is clearly nervous, because he has just given up three hits in a row, and now the largest kid in the universe is standing in the batter's box. All the other kids and our fans are probably praying, "Come on, Garth! Please just get this one hit!"

I know I am. If Garth wins the game, I will be saved from having to bat with everyone depending on me. But Garth hits a super-high pop-up in the infield that gets caught by the second baseman. When Scott limps up to the plate, several kids on our team actually groan out loud. Then it gets incredibly quiet as the pitcher winds up, except for the voice of Scott's dad, who helpfully shouts, "Come *on*, Scott! Be a winner!" He doesn't add *for once*, but the tone of his voice makes the meaning pretty clear.

Scott swings super hard at three pitches in a row but never even makes contact with the ball. Great! Now I am up with the bases loaded and two outs. If I get on, we have a chance. If I get out, we lose. I crowd the plate as much as I possibly can—my toes are actually touching the white inside line of the batter's box. I am leaning out so far over the plate that I feel like I might lose my balance and fall.

I don't swing at the first pitch, a called strike. I could have swung, but the pitch looked a bit low to me, and hitting a weak little grounder would be a sure way to lose us the game. The next three pitches are balls, which makes the count 3–1. According to all the wisdom of a hundred years of baseball, I should be in a perfect position to hit right now, because the pitcher can't afford to walk me, which means his next pitch should be right down the middle. It is, but I don't swing. I am just praying for ball four.

The umpire looks at me with what I swear is disgust. "Come on, kid, swing the bat," he mutters. This doesn't seem promising.

I hear my father in the stands say, "You can do this, Jord!"

Sadly, he is wrong. The next pitch is completely out of the strike zone, so low that it hits the ground before it reaches the catcher. But I am convinced that the ump will call any pitch a strike at this point if I don't swing, so I take a wild, lunging hack at the ball and miss by about six inches.

Game over. On the way back to the dugout, I get booed by my own team. I do not enjoy it.

Getting into the car, my father says, "It's okay, you'll get them next time!" He has no idea how right he is.

Every Monday at school, there is a group of boys who rush to gather together and discuss the skits from that week's *Saturday Night Live*. We talk about what was funny, what was stupid, and what *we* would have done if we had been in charge of writing the script. Miss Tuff must have noticed our little get-togethers, because the Monday after my cartoon incident and the pathetic baseball game, she calls three of us up to her desk during silent-reading time. There's Jonathan Marks, Joey Chablis, and me.

"Boys," she says, "I have an idea. How would you like to write a few skits of your own and then perform them for the class?"

Jonathan, Joey, and I look at one another in amazement. How would we like it? She might as well have asked us how we would like a million bucks each, or unlimited pizza at lunch. This is too good to be true. I have spent my whole school career getting in trouble whenever I try to make the class laugh, and now Miss Tuff is asking us to make the class laugh as an assignment!

We spend all our free time for the next week huddled in the janitor's broom closet across the hall, frantically brainstorming and writing until we have three full skits, a song, and a pretend commercial. The closet is kind of dark and super damp. The mop bucket smells awful, like there is something dead floating in the water. And yet, I have never had a better time in school. By Friday, we are ready to perform for the class.

We have written in a surprise for Miss Tuff, too. At lunch, we tell all our classmates that they will have a job to do during the last skit, and they get pretty psyched about it.

The first skit goes great. Then we do our song. There has been a huge news story this week about how 273 people were killed in the crash of American Airlines Flight 191, making it the worst accident in the history of US air flight. The plane was a DC-10, and the newspapers say that DC-10s are the most dangerous aircraft in America.

Clearly, this is a comedy goldmine.

The song is modeled after John Denver's hit "Leaving on a Jet Plane."

We sing,

"I'm flyin' on a DC-10,
Don't know if I'll be back again
Depends on whether they inspected the plane!"

This is a huge hit with the class. We are on a roll, and the second skit goes great, too. All we have left is our commercial, followed by the secret-class-participation finale. The commercial is a parody of the popular Irish Spring soap commercial, which features a woman whistling at a man like she is admiring his looks. Then the man looks right at the camera and says, "Irish Spring—it gets you fresh and clean as a whistle!"

Jonathan and I, who are both Jewish, have come up with a slightly different version. We have wrapped a bar of soap in plain white paper, and then decorated the outside with a big Star of David. Jonathan walks across the front of the room holding up the soap bar, and Joey whistles at him. Then Jonathan looks out over the class and says, "Jewish Spring— it's kosher for Passover!"

Everybody laughs at this line, and a feeling flows over me that I have never felt before. The class is cracking up over a joke I wrote, and I *am not getting in trouble for it.* When I look over at Miss Tuff, she is beaming with pride. I feel powerful! My words are controlling my class! I almost feel like I am getting away with something. *This* is what I want to do with my life.

The last skit is even better. It has two things going on at once. I am pretending to be the teacher, and Jonathan and Joey, along with the rest of the kids in the room, are supposed to be my class. I start teaching a math lesson, but that is just an excuse for the *real* skit. Every time I call on a kid and ask for the answer to a problem I've written on the board, that student asks, "May I go to the bathroom?" Each time, I sigh and say, "Yes."

Within a few minutes, every kid in the class is gone, except for Jonathan, Joey, and me. I glance over at Miss Tuff, and see that she looks baffled and kind of concerned. I dismiss Jonathan to the bathroom. I dismiss Joey to the bathroom.

Now it's just Miss Tuff and me in the room. I turn to her, raise my hand, and ask, "May I go to the bathroom?"

She must be dying to know what's going on, but she doesn't say that. She just tells me I can go, although she does follow me to the classroom door. As I step through the doorway into the hall—where everybody I've dismissed is crouching against the wall—the whole class breaks out in giggles.

Miss Tuff sees what is going on, and after a second, she starts clapping.

I am a star. No, better than that: I am a *writer.*

23. The Dark Is Rising, and So Am I

B.J. and I have always shared books. I discovered comics first, when we were in first grade and my dad's barber had *Avengers #138* (*Stranger in a Strange Man!*) and *Daredevil #112* (*"Murder!" Cries the Mandrill!*). B.J. got me into DC Comics last year, when he discovered the Legion of Super-Heroes. I lend him my science fiction novels, and he brings me piles of fantasy books. We spend hours on top of his bunk bed arguing over who would win in different battles. Would Shazam beat Thor? What would happen if Gandalf from Lord of the Rings fought Darth Vader? Could Saturn Girl from the Legion of Super-Heroes read Professor Xavier's mind?

These arguments get pretty heated. I once got sent home by B.J.'s mom when B.J. and I started wrestling to decide whether Superboy was stronger than Ultra Boy. The issue was very complicated, because we had a list of each hero's powers, and we saw that Ultra Boy had invulnerability. We didn't know what that was. We couldn't even pronounce it. So when B.J. said Superboy was probably stronger than Ultra Boy, there was only one way to figure it out. I jumped on him and shouted, "Invability! I win!" He yelled, "Heat vision! You lose!" I got him in a headlock and shouted, "Invability beats heat vision!" He rolled over so he was on top of me and grunted, "Super breath!"

Which has to be Superboy's dumbest power, by the way.

This went back and forth for a while, but eventually B.J. pushed me against the wall with his feet. I grabbed B.J.'s gold necklace, pulled on it, and screamed, "Invability!" B.J. pushed off from me so he was hanging halfway off the bed. Then his necklace broke and he fell.

He wasn't even hurt, but his mom was super mad! She said his necklace, which had the Hebrew symbol Chai on it for good luck, was a family heirloom, whatever that means. The next thing I knew, I was sitting in my mom's car on the way home, getting yelled at by her, too.

Apparently, super mad beats invability.

B.J. and I might get into some heated debates once in a while, but aside from being the smartest kid I know, he also has amazing taste. So one day, when he brings in a new book for me to read and says I have to drop everything and start it right away, I listen. The book is by an author I've never heard of named Susan Cooper, and it's called *The Dark Is Rising*.

Fantasy books always sound kind of stupid when you try to explain them. I know this because Lissa points it out to me often. So I will just say that this one is about a boy named Will Stanton, who finds out on his eleventh birthday that he has secret magical powers that set him apart from humanity. If he has the courage, wits, and honor to defeat a terrible, ancient threat, the world will be saved. If he doesn't, we are all doomed.

I like most fantasy books well enough, but *The Dark Is Rising* changes my life. I can't stop reading it! I make my mom take me to the library right away to get the next three books. For two weeks, I feel like I am living three lives: I am a Jewish kid living in Staten Island, but I am also an English country boy who is *also* a magical being. Half my head is in New York City, but the other half is in Great Britain. Whenever I close my eyes, I am Will Stanton, wandering the back lanes of Buckinghamshire and the hills of Wales, facing evil horsemen and gigantic gray foxes, and hunting for magical weapons to use against the Dark.

Will has exactly what I've always wanted. He is special and needed. And like the best kind of magic, reading his story gives me the strength to stop pulling my hair out. I mean, if Will Stanton doesn't tear his hair out when a terrible, supernatural blizzard cuts his village off from the world, or when his mother falls down the basement steps and breaks her leg, or when his sister gets kidnapped by the awful Masters of the Dark, I figure I should be able to handle my worries without attacking my own head.

I have tried hard to stop before, but I know this time, I'm stopping for good.

When I finish reading the last book in the series, *Silver on the Tree*, I have a totally unheard-of reaction to it being over: I cry. I am so happy that Will and his friends have saved the world, but also completely crushed that our adventure together is over.

This is what I want to write when I grow up. I want to write books that make other kids feel just like Will Stanton. I want other kids to know they are special and needed, too.

I am so special and needed that I get traded away from my own baseball team.

No, it's worse than that: I get *given* away by my own baseball team.

At the game after my terrible bases-loaded strikeout, Lockwood Plumbing shows up at the field and finds that the other team, Behrins' Bullets, has only six players. Mr. Dave offers to lend the other coach three of our players so the game doesn't have to be canceled.

Naturally, he picks his three worst guys: Garth, Scott, and me. Walking from our dugout across the field is the worst feeling in the world. I am super sad but also super mad. I feel like I am going to cry, but there is no freaking way I can show any sign of tears on this field. Garth turns to me on the bench, where the three of us are sitting all the way at one end, and says, "We have to win this game."

Heck yeah, we do.

Nick the super-fastball pitcher is on the mound for our team—well, our old team. He hasn't lost a single game all year, but when I step into the batter's box in the third inning as the number-seven batter in the Behrins' Bullets lineup, I realize I am not scared of him. First of all, even though he throws very hard, he only has one pitch. Second of all, I know he has great control, because he hasn't walked or hit anybody all season. So I tell myself two things: I don't have to be afraid, and I am not getting on base unless I hit the ball. I get the team's first hit of the day with a grounder up the third-base line. Then I steal second base.

Lockwood Plumbing scores a couple of runs, but Behrins' Bullets starts hitting in the fifth inning. I come up to bat with a guy on second and two outs. Nick glares like he is absolutely furious at me—like I *betrayed my own team* by getting a hit. Well, tough. My team shouldn't have dumped me.

Garrett, the catcher, shouts to Nick, "Easy out!" On any other day, he would be right, but not today. I foul off the first pitch, and the second pitch is a called strike. But I know the third pitch is going to be right down the middle. I swing with all my might and connect!

Okay, so the ball rolls about eleven feet up the first-base line and dies. But still, Nick hasn't struck me out. The catcher pops up from his crouch, grabs the ball, and throws it to first, but his throw is super high. It bangs off the far edge of the wooden frame of the Behrins' Bullets dugout and keeps going into the outfield. I take off for second base and slide just as the throw from right field sails over the shortstop's head. As I pop up, the third baseman runs into short left field to get the ball, and I realize there's nobody to cover third. I take off again. Just as I slide into third, the pitcher realizes what's going on and charges over. The third baseman throws the ball right to the base, but the pitcher isn't there yet, and it flies over me and bangs off the fence of the Lockwood Plumbing dugout.

I head for home plate, where Garrett is crouched, ready to catch the ball and also hurt me. I slide between his legs as the throw gets to him. I hit him so hard he drops the ball. He still tags me on the side of the head really hard just because he *can*, but I don't care. I get up before he does, step over his legs, and practically glide back to the dugout. Everybody there is jumping up and down. It's 2–2, and I have just come the closest I ever will to hitting a home run. As Scott limps past me to bat, we smile at each other. Garth is swinging two bats in the on-deck circle. I reach up, slap him on the shoulder, and say, "You're gonna hit a homer." He laughs, but I am totally serious.

Nick is so rattled, he walks Scott.

Garth looks into the dugout, where I am up on my feet with everybody else, screaming and shaking the fence. We make eye contact, and I can see it. Garth has already gotten banished by his own team. He has nothing left to lose, and he's mad. He really *is* going to hit a home run!

And he does.

On the very first pitch, he absolutely creams the ball out over the right fielder's head. Our home field doesn't have an outfield fence. The grass just ends maybe twenty feet past where the outfielders usually stand. In right field, that's where a deep, mucky swamp starts. In three years of playing right field, I have never seen a ball roll into the swamp.

Garth's shot gets there on the fly. The right fielder wades in to retrieve it.

Garth chugs up the baseline as fast as he can, which isn't saying much. It does mean he nearly catches up to Scott between second and third, though. I look into the outfield and see that the right fielder has found the ball. He hurls it to the second baseman, who makes a perfect relay throw home.

Scott crosses the plate while the ball is still in the air, but Garrett catches it when Garth is still a couple of steps away. All he has to do is tag Garth and hold on to the ball to keep the game tied up. But this is Garth we are talking about. He's like six feet tall and two hundred pounds, and he is charging down the line like an enraged bull.

Garrett steps aside and tries to tag Garth's back. He misses. Both dugouts erupt. The Lockwood Plumbing players are calling Garth a traitor. The Behrins' Bullets guys are all waiting in line to give Garth high fives. When he gets to me, we hug.

"Told ya," I say.

Our new team scores another couple of runs in the sixth, and we become the first team to beat Lockwood Plumbing in a game started by Nick. At the end, we line up to shake hands. I have to admit, that is kind of awkward for Garth, Scott, and me, now that everyone on Lockwood Plumbing except Pete wants to kill us.

When I get to Pete, he raises one eyebrow and says, "Really?"

Okay, even Pete wants to kill us a *little*.

24. A Tough Time

June is weird. On the one hand, we have an awesome Field Day, I am the rabbi at a wedding, and my mom brings me home an awesome surprise! On the other hand, the world almost ends again.

My mom has been having all kinds of problems with her new car. It makes alarming noises, it stalls at random times, and no matter how many times Sam and Nick fix it, nothing helps for long. My parents have been saying the car is a lemon, which seems to be like a bad egg but with wheels. This has made driving very adventurous already, but then things get a lot worse.

I guess some country called Iran, which has a lot of oil, had a revolution. Now they aren't making oil, or they aren't selling oil, or we aren't buying their oil—I don't exactly understand what's going on, but my dad says this could mean the end of civilization. For me, what it means is that there's a sudden gasoline shortage in Staten Island. It gets so bad that the whole city of New York makes a crazy rule that people can only buy gas for their cars every other day. If your car's license plates end in an odd number, you can buy on the odd-numbered days of the month. If it ends in an even number, you can buy on the even-numbered days. But this doesn't solve the crisis, because so many people line up every day that the gas stations all run out of fuel by noon or so.

This means that when my mom needs gas, she wakes me and Lissa up in the middle of the night. First, we get dressed and brush our teeth. Next, we take pillows and blankets, climb into the hatchback part of the Citation with the back seats folded down, and try to get back to sleep while Mom drives over to Sam & Nick's and parks behind the last car in line to wait for the pumps to open in the morning. It's unbelievable. Usually when we get there, the line is already like half a block long!

We really do try to sleep, but it's hard. There's brightness from the city streetlights pouring into the windows, and bunches of grown-ups are standing outside their cars, talking and smoking cigarettes. Plus, the back of the car isn't as comfy as a real bed. By seven in the morning, when the gas station opens, my mom has generally scolded us a bunch of times for whispering and laughing.

When the car starts moving, we give up on sleep, sit up, and eat a couple of Pop-Tarts for breakfast. If she isn't too annoyed, Mom gives us money to run over to the soda machine. Coke and a Pop-Tart is basically the perfect breakfast, so that is kind of fun. Then, once the gas tank is full, we drive to I.S. 27 to drop Lissa off before heading over to the Staten Island Expressway and P.S. 54.

By the time I get to school, I have already been awake for hours and hours. So have probably half the other kids in my class, but it doesn't stop us from being wildly excited for what everyone says is the best day of the year: Field Day. This is way better than the stupid maypole decoration ceremony we used to have every spring at P.S. 35. Field Day is basically a mini-Olympics, and each class is like one of the countries. In Miss Tuff's room, we come up with a team slogan: "You'll have a tough time with TUFF'S TEAM!" Then a group of kids who are good at art make a T-shirt design on a rectangle of cardboard. Once that is done, each kid in the class has to bring in a plain white T-shirt, stick the cardboard rectangle between the front and back of the shirt, and use markers to trace the design onto it, so that we all have matching TUFF'S TEAM shirts.

Well, that's the plan. Mine comes out with big blobs of ink everywhere because I forget to keep my marker moving while I am tracing the design. And one side of my rectangular design is outlined much more thickly than the other, because I panicked halfway through and decided the line on that side looked too thin. I look around, and everybody else's shirts look pretty much identical. Mine looks recognizable. If you squint kind of hard. I *hope*.

By the time the week of Field Day comes, all the classes are going wild with excitement. Miss Tuff has bet one of the other fourth-grade teachers that our class will beat the other teacher's class, and Miss Tuff is super serious about the bet. We even have several practices. I am in the three-legged race, the potato sack relay, and the two most important events of all: the 50-yard-dash relay and the tug o' war.

When Miss Tuff hands out the roster sheet, I have no idea what a three-legged race is. I have a partner for it, though, so maybe she knows. Her name is Michelle Longo, and she is very tan, very pretty, and very tall. I ask her, and she totally does know. Apparently, we are going to stand next to each other while somebody ties my left leg to her right leg. Then we will have to run together like we were one person, but with three legs.

I don't know how to feel about this. For one thing, Michelle is so pretty that I can't look at her without blushing, and every time I have to talk to her I start sweating and sound like an idiot. This is complicated by the height difference. How are we going to run together when our legs are completely different lengths? Are they going to have to tie my thigh to her knee?

I find out at practice. First, they tie our ankles together with a short piece of rope. Then they use another piece to tie our upper legs together. It's not quite as bad as I had imagined. The rope goes around my thigh, but crosses around Michelle's leg a couple of inches above her knee.

But once my leg is tied to Michelle's, skin to skin, I am terrified. What if I sweat? What if she is disgusted by my incredible amount of leg hair? (I am seriously hairy—kids have been calling me Monkey Arms since second grade.) What if I am slower than she is?

And where the heck am I supposed to put my left arm?

Before I can quite figure this out, someone shouts, "Go!"

Michelle lunges forward, which *hurts*. I can feel the rope tearing out my leg hairs! When she realizes she is dragging me, she says, "Let's *go*!" and throws her right arm around my neck to keep me with her. I fling my left arm around her back. Now she has me in some kind of wrestling hold, and I have my hand on her waist.

This would be a good time for me to suddenly get tall.

I start stepping at top speed, but by the time we are halfway to the finish line, another problem comes up: We are gradually turning right because my strides are so much shorter

than hers. I try to turn us back on course by hurling my right leg forward each time, but this makes me turn inward toward Michelle. Somehow, our feet get tangled up so we fall on our faces.

Michelle turns to me, her eyes inches from mine. I wait for her to scream at me from point-blank range. Instead, she laughs!

"That wasn't . . . smooth," I manage to sputter, before I start laughing, too. By the time we somehow coordinate ourselves so we can stand up together, I have learned one important fact: I *love* Field Day, and it hasn't even happened yet.

Potato sack relay practice gives me another chance to prove my athletic grace. I step into one of the two moldy-smelling cloth bags that Miss Tuff has placed on the ground at the starting line, and pull the top of the bag up above my waist with both hands when I see our class's other potato sack racer, Ramesh, do the same. I bet these bags were chosen with taller kids in mind, because in order to keep the bottom of mine pulled tight against my feet, I have to hold my hands practically up to my chin. I must look like a miniature *Tyrannosaurus* with my arms bent up in front of me, but the good news is that this comes in handy when I fall on my face yet again halfway to the finish line. My hands take the impact, and I scramble back to my feet in time to complete the race.

Ramesh is already standing just past the line, holding his bag at arm's length and grinning. *Well*, I tell myself, *second place isn't bad.*

In the 50-yard-dash relay, I am one of four boys competing for our class. Miss Tuff hands the front boy the shiny, hollow metal baton, and then arranges the rest of us in order. I am third in line, between Ramesh and—eek!—Albert. What if Albert purposely crashes into me when I hand him the shiny, hollow metal baton? What if he trips me? Or, worst of all, what if he yells at me in front of everybody for being slow?

We practice the relay three times. The first time, Miss Tuff has each of us jog so we can get used to handing off the baton at a slow speed. The second time, we try it faster, and I drop the baton when Ramesh slaps it into my hand. The third time, Albert pretends he is going to trip me. He doesn't *actually* trip me, and he kind of smiles at me as he pulls his foot back.

Maybe I will survive the real race. That would be nice.

My final event, the tug o' war, will also be the final event of the real Field Day. Miss Tuff tells us we will need to give this contest our all, because it is worth a lot of points and usually determines the winner of the entire thing.

No pressure.

The big, fat, heavy old rope is lying on the ground across a spray-painted red stripe. Miss Tuff explains that in order to win, we have to pull the rope until the other team gets pulled all the way across the red stripe. If we get pulled across the stripe first, then we lose. That seems simple enough until we try it.

The first thing we need to figure out is who will be our "anchor person." That's the kid at the very end of the rope, behind the rest of us. There is a person-sized loop at each end of the rope, and the anchor person has to step into the loop and pick up the rope before the rest of us grab on. Being the anchor looks scary, because that is the one kid who can't let go of the rope. If another team is much stronger than ours, I figure there is a pretty good chance the anchor kid will go flying, and maybe even get dragged on the ground.

Luckily, there is no chance I will be the anchor. We have to choose either the biggest kid or the strongest for that position.

For once, I am glad to be tiny and weak.

The biggest kid is Chuck Dai and the strongest is Walter P. Kelly. In order to figure out who should be the anchor, Miss Tuff has us practice against the rest of the class twice. The result is that we decide our smartest lineup has Chuck in the anchor position, with Walter P. at the very front. Also, I get a blister.

But we are ready for the big day. That's good, because nobody can talk about anything else. I would not have imagined there could be so much debate over proper egg-spoon relay technique or water-balloon toss strategies. It is amazing: Kids have theories about everything. Which partner should go on the ground first for the wheelbarrow race? Somebody has a formula.

My big Field Day goals are to not lose any teeth, not embarrass myself to death, and maybe even stay on my feet the majority of the time. I have dreams of winning ribbons and helping Tuff's Team to victory, but I'll definitely settle for the keeping of teeth, the non-embarrassment, and the remaining upright.

The weekend before the big event, Peter comes over after a Little League game. We are playing with Hectoria and J.P. when we get an idea. The snakes have been hanging all over each other ever since the day J.P. first joined my family, and I am about to go away to camp for eight weeks. Peter, who's going for a second summer, too, says Hectoria might get pregnant again while we are gone, and that seems weird to us. I mean, I made them live together, and they are clearly more than friends. The least we can do is make their relationship official.

The only thing to do is perform a wedding ceremony for the two snakes.

This is serious business, and it has to be done right. I go up into the attic and get the spare aquarium that has been empty ever since the brutal murder of Stripe. We pour in half a bag of fresh, new pebbles from the pet store. Then we need guests and an altar. I am a little bit stumped when it comes to the guest list, because our only other pets are Spicy, who is too big to fit, and Freddie the Second, who is clearly not an option. We settle on making two lines of my action figures, plus some Barbies stolen from Lissa's closet. We push the dolls' feet down into the pebbles until they are all standing up, facing each other across the aisle. Superman, Batman, Aquaman, the Flash, and two G.I. Joes are on one side, and all the Barbies are on the other.

The altar is a tough choice. Pete and I are both Jewish, but J.P. is kind of named after a pope. Do we go Jewish or Catholic for this thing? After a brief argument, we realize we don't have anything Catholic anyway. The only solemn-seeming item of any kind in my whole room is a souvenir miniature totem pole that my grandparents once brought me from Canada. We plant it at the front of the aisle.

Next, Peter and I both put yarmulkes on our heads. They are a tasteful deep-maroon velvet and are left over from my cousin Marc's bar mitzvah.

The only last detail is the music for when Hecky and J.P. slither down the aisle. I feel it has to be a Beatles song. I have a new album, *1962–66*, which Mr. Stoll has lent me, plus my parents have bought me *The Beatles at the Hollywood Bowl*. At first, I think of the most romantic Beatles song I know: "I Want to Hold Your Hand." But Peter feels that would be kind of mean, since snakes don't have hands. We go with my second choice, "She's a Woman," from the Hollywood Bowl record. This makes good sense, because you can hear a crowd cheering through the entire thing. Hopefully, that will make Hecky and J.P. feel supported in their new life together.

When we think everything is ready, I put the needle down on the record, and we place the snakes at the beginning of the aisle. Then disaster strikes! J.P. doesn't want to move, and Hecky immediately wraps herself around Batman.

It's a nightmare.

I pick the needle up, and we get the snakes pointed in the right direction again. This time, J.P. turns completely around and starts trying to climb the glass at the back of the aisle, while Hecky cuddles up to Stewardess Barbie.

I am starting to wonder whether these snakes even *want* to make a commitment.

Before the third try, we take out all the dolls, push most of the rocks out of the center of the cage so there's a canyon to guide the snakes, replant the dolls, and give Hecky and J.P. a pep talk.

It works! They glide directly to the front and start climbing the totem pole.

I make my voice as deep as I can and say the first Hebrew thing that comes to me, which is "Baruch Atah Adonai Eloheinu Melech ha'olam ha'motzi lechem min ha'aretz." Technically, I have just blessed any bread that might be nearby, but it will have to do.

Pete and I place the bride and groom back in their own tank and leave them to enjoy their honeymoon. Then we go downstairs and have some Twinkies. Hey, those are kind of like bread! If the drumming and the writing don't work out, I think I show some promise as a rabbi.

Field Day gets postponed due to rain, which makes that Monday the worst Monday in the history of Mondays. But the weather forecast is good for Tuesday, so that's when the event finally happens. Things start out great for Tuff's Team.

In the egg-spoon relay, powered by B.J.'s tremendous last lap, we win by a mile. In the water-balloon toss, Chandra and Mondhipa come in second. Jonathan Marks and Stu Heffer (slogan: "Pee-wee power!") absolutely crush the opposition in the wheelbarrow race.

A few events later, Michelle and I are tied together and lined up for the three-legged race. Miss Tuff has shared a brilliant last-minute tip with us. Apparently, the key to not falling on our faces is keeping our strides together, so she says we should chant, "Out, in, out, in" as we step with our outside legs and then our inside ones. We have taken a few practice strides, and I am pretty sure we know what we are doing, although this doesn't do anything to stop the cords from ripping out the hairs on my legs.

"Okay," Michelle says, looking me in the eyes. "No laughing, right?"

"Right," I say. Then we both start giggling.

But hey—we do the "out, in" chanting trick, and it basically works. We still turn off course a bit because my legs are just too short, but we come in third. That's good enough for a ribbon! I am a bit sad when we get untied, because I think we could totally come in second if we had one more chance at this thing.

On the other hand, maybe it is good to quit while I still have some leg hair left.

In the potato sack race, I get an amazing start. I am leaping my heart out. I look around and realize I am in the lead. I have pulled away from everybody! Then I twist my left ankle by hitting a little hole in the grass of the field, fall sideways, and take out two other racers. But it's all good, because Ramesh hops right over our bodies and into a first-place finish.

That is totally worth a bit of ankle pain and a faceful of dirt.

I barely have time to swish a cup of water around my mouth to get the soil out of my front teeth before we have to line up for the 50-yard-dash relay. Today, our team's baton is a very bright neon green. *Well*, I think, *at least it will be easy to find if I drop it!*

But I don't drop it. When Ramesh hands the baton to me, we are in first place. All I have to do is keep the lead and then make a smooth handoff to Albert, who's super fast. I pump my legs as fast as I can, trying to ignore the little twinges of pain from my twisted ankle. I run the first twenty-five yards, run around the cone there, and sprint back toward my team. "Hurry UP!" Albert is screaming, over and over.

I do my best, but one kid passes me just before I reach Albert. "Go, go, go!" everybody shouts at him as I press the baton into his hand and fall over into the grass, panting. Albert goes, goes, goes, and passes the other kid about ten feet before he gets back to our line. We all jump up and down like maniacs! Albert even gives me a high five.

It's crazy. If you had told me back in April that Albert and I would be trading high fives two months later, I would have laughed in your face. But now it's different, because now I am a part of Tuff's Team.

We are within just a few points of two other teams when the tug o' war comes around. There are two elimination rounds, and then the team that comes out on top of those has one final battle against the team that has the most points going into the event. So we will need to win three matches in a row in order to win the whole Field Day.

We win the first round pretty easily. I am near the front of our line, just behind Walter P., and I can see the moment very clearly when all the members of the other team suddenly start tumbling forward. Then they all let go of the rope so fast that we all fall backward onto our butts. We are victorious! And our tushies are grass stained!

Our second round is harder. When Walter P. sees how big and strong-looking the kids on the other end of the rope are, he calls a quick huddle. We decide that Walter P. should go to the back of the line, just in front of Chuck, so we will almost have two anchor guys. That leaves me at the very front, staring at the determined faces of our opponents. We pick up the rope, and when the teacher says "Go!" we pull as hard as we can. Unfortunately, the ground under our feet is now all torn up and muddy from the first two sets of teams digging their feet into it. I can hear the other team grunting as my feet begin to slide toward them.

In desperation, I turn around so I am facing back at my own team. I dig my toes into the mucky ground with all my might, put the rope over my shoulder, and pull like I am trying to burst into a sprint. The rope stops moving. Then it slowly begins to come our way. "Pull!" Chuck yells.

I'm not sure what he thinks we've been doing—reading the newspaper?

But we pull and pull, until again, there is a sudden slack in the rope as the other team lets go. Now I have a mud-covered front to match my grassy butt.

Just before the championship round, Chuck pulls up his shirt and we all see that he has rope burns all around the back of his waist. Walter P. switches spots with him, and as we all pick up the rope, they both nod at the rest of us. This is it! Off to one side, I see Miss Tuff smiling at us in encouragement. We have to win this for her.

We don't. Instead, we all lose our footing almost right away, and even when I turn my back on the other team, I can't get my feet to grip. I feel myself being marched backward toward the other team, and there is nothing I can do to stop it. Someone near the back starts chanting, "Heave! Heave!"—but you can't heave when you can't stand. Thanks to Louise Boily, I refuse to let go of the rope, so I get dragged across the middle ground on my chest.

That's okay. My shirt art was pretty terrible, anyway.

But I can't believe we have lost! We were so close!

As the tug o' war team limps our way back to the rest of the class, B.J. says, "Great effort, guys!" I want to shout and stomp. I want to curse at the sky! It wasn't a great effort, because we *lost*.

But then Miss Tuff calls us all together into a huddle. We all have our arms around one another, and as we lean in, she says, "I am *so* proud of all of you. You are the *best*! Now, on the count of three, I want you to all yell, 'TUFF'S TEAM!' One, two, three!"

I shout so hard that it feels like my throat is tearing. When I catch Miss Tuff's eye, she smiles, just at me. Then she moves her head slowly from one end of the huddle to the other. I think she is trying to smile at each kid in the class, one at a time. She really *is* proud of us.

Maybe I didn't really lose today. I mean, I *definitely* lost a tug o' war. And a T-shirt. But I gained a *team*.

25. The Packing List

I spend the end of June packing for camp and panicking. What if camp isn't as amazing this year as it was last year? Will Hecky and J.P. be okay without me? And when I get back, how am I going to survive fifth grade without Miss Tuff?

My room looks like the staging area for a military attack. There are piles of stuff on every surface, including the floor, and nothing can be moved into my huge, open camp trunk until my mom has checked it off. Here is the camp packing list:

```
8-10 pair long pants-sweats, jeans, etc.      2 pair sneakers
8-10 pair shorts                              1 pair flip flop rubber
15 t-shirts, ect.                                 sandals
4-6 long sleeved sweatshirts, shirts or       12 towels
        lighter jackets                       washcloths
1 warmer jacket                               3 warm blankets
16 pairs of underwear                         sleeping bag
16 pairs of sox                               dufflebag
3 pairs of pajamas                            pillow
bathrobe
3 bathing suits(quick-dry material)           tennis racquet
raincoat with hat or hood                     1 can of tennis balls
pair of rainy-day footwear                    softball glove
a pair of OLD sneakers for canoe trips        baseball cap
```

```
  A supply of the usual toilet articles that the camper uses:
toothbrush, toothpaste, comb, brush, soap, nail file or clippers,
drinking cup, tissues, ect. in a carrying case. Put names on all
items.
```

All that stuff takes up a lot of space. Also, we have to label everything with my name, which takes *forever*. That is a super-important step, though, because everything from all the boys in my cabin will get thrown into one huge laundry bag each week, and if my stuff isn't labeled, there will be no way for me to get it back when the laundry returns a week later. Last year, Paul Golin almost ended up with my Yankees shirt, with Ron Guidry's name on the back. That would have been an epic tragedy, in my opinion.

Also, I am completely sure that Michael Fein went home with my toothbrush AND my collapsible drinking cup.

Slowly, the piles get moved into the trunk. My baseball mitt can't go in until the last minute because I am going to a Yankees game with Peter Friedman and another kid named Billy Burns the day before we leave. We do this every year for Pete's birthday, and our seats are always in the upper deck where the ball never goes—but I am not taking any chances. If there is the slightest possibility of catching a real baseball that has been touched by real Yankees, I need that glove.

As my mom is looking over everything three days before the beginning of camp, I make her go over all the snake-care plans. Does she remember where to buy the fish for them to eat? Does she remember the schedule? Does she promise she will change the water in their bowl at least once a week? Will she take their skins out of the tank if they shed?

Will she hold them so they don't get too lonely or sad?

This is when my mother does something great. She goes downstairs, gets our Kodak disc camera, and takes a few photos of Hecky and J.P. She swears she will get the film developed in time for me to take the photos to camp.

Once we are done with this first round of packing, my mom tells me that she and my dad have decided to give me my birthday present early. I was born on the Fourth of July, which means I will be at camp for the real day, so this makes sense. At dinner, my parents tell me to close my eyes. When I open them, there is a gift on the table in front of me. It's big.

I tear the wrapping paper off. Inside is a cardboard box that says D'AGOSTINO DRUMS. My heart pounding, I rip the flaps of the box open. Inside is a beautiful, shiny black snare drum.

I can't believe it! I must be a real drummer now, because I have a real drum! I hug my parents so hard it is a miracle that their ribs don't break. Then I ask to be excused, run to grab my best pair of nylon-tipped Fibes 5As, and charge back into the kitchen. Pulling the drum out, I ask my mom where the stand for it is.

She looks confused. "There's supposed to be . . . a stand?" she asks.

I try not to sound sad as I say, "Don't worry about it. The drum is *perfect*! Thank you!"

Then, with my parents watching, I balance the drum on my lap and play my best long roll. It still doesn't quite sound like paper tearing, but I'm pretty sure my hands are starting to look a bit blurry.

At the Yankee game, Peter's parents buy food and programs for everybody, and then lead Pete, Billy Burns, and me to three seats way up high above first base. Then they tell us their seats are two sections away from ours. Billy, Pete, and I can't believe it! We are on our own at Yankee Stadium!

As the Yankees begin their batting practice, the three of us dig into our hot dogs and French fries, gulp down our huge Cokes, and practice our burping skills. When our meal is finished, we have a bunch of unused ketchup packets. This gives us an idea. Pete's fifth-grade teacher, Mr. Lord, did a whole unit on flight, which included a big lab project on making paper planes. We start ripping pages out of our programs and folding them into a little air force. When our little fleet is assembled, each of us carefully rips open a ketchup packet, sticks it in the center crease of a plane, and then throws it as far as we can out over the edge of the upper deck.

This is super fun. And the best part is, we still have enough ketchup to launch at least three more missions!

As the teams line up along the basepaths for the national anthem, a huge, muscular man in a sleeveless T-shirt comes storming out of the stairwell next to our section. The T-shirt probably started the day being totally white. Now it has a surprisingly large patch of red on the front.

Heinz red.

The guy starts yelling, "Who's been throwing ketchup off the upper deck? Huh? Huh?"

Peter, Billy, and I shrink down into our seats. I wait for some other fan nearby to point us out to the guy. Nobody does, though, and after what feels like the longest half minute of my life, the guy ends his speech with "I better not see anything else flying down from here! *You hear me?*"

We hear him. Half the *city* hears him.

By the third inning, the three of us are laughing about this so hard that tears actually roll down Billy's cheek, and I can't even catch my breath. But on the way home, I replay the whole scene in my head, and I can't stop thinking that the guy had to sit through the whole game with ketchup all over him. Maybe he is on a subway right now, still covered with it, and everybody is staring.

When I get home, I shove my game program into the bottom drawer of my desk. I don't like seeing the gap where the missing pages should be. I almost tell my parents what we've done, but instead, I just keep seeing it in my head over and over again that night when I am trying to sleep.

I am confused. Sometimes, it's really hard to figure out when having fun is just fun, and when it is the same as being bad.

The next morning, I throw my glove on top of the pile, and the entire packing list is completely checked off. I am ready to slam the trunk shut and put on the big, heavy combination lock when my mother realizes I don't have everything I need.

"Jord, the pictures!" she cries.

How could I have forgotten Hecky? I run downstairs, where the envelope of developed film is sitting on the kitchen table. A lot of the shots are pretty blurry and dark, but there is one that's perfect. Hecky's tongue is flickered out, and J.P. has his head on her back. When I look at it, I can almost imagine my snakes are *moving*. I dig around in my father's desk for an empty envelope, put that picture in, and go back upstairs. After I tuck the envelope into the webbing of my baseball glove, my mom starts to close the trunk.

"Wait!" I say. There are a couple of other things I can't go eight weeks without. I run over to the bookshelf that hangs over my head when I am in bed and grab *The Dark Is Rising*, along with a few of my newest, most exciting comics. I know I will have a much better time at Rest Hour each day if I can reread *The Avengers Annual #9*. And *Uncanny X-Men #121*. And *The Amazing Spider-Man #194*.

I place the comics carefully between two thick sweatshirts for maximum protection.

Now there is only one thing left that I can't live without: the drums. There's no room for a whole snare drum in my trunk, plus my mom points out that the other kids in my cabin would probably want to kill me if I spent Rest Hours pounding on it and chanting, "Ma-ma-da-da, ma-ma-da-da." I can see her point, so I just throw in my comfiest pair of Fibes 5As, followed by the dictionary, which fits perfectly right on top of the two sneaker boxes in the front left-hand corner.

I nod at my mother. She closes the trunk, and I snap on the lock.

I have books. I have music. I am ready for anything.

ABOUT THE AUTHOR

Before Jordan Sonnenblick was an author, teacher, parent, and adult, he was a kid who liked drums, snakes, jokes, and baseball . . . which is what this book is about. His many acclaimed novels include *The Secret Sheriff of Sixth Grade*; *Drums, Girls, and Dangerous Pie*; *After Ever After*; *Notes from the Midnight Driver*; and *Falling Over Sideways*. He lives in Bethlehem, Pennsylvania with his family. You can find out more about him at jordansonnenblick.com.

Sixth grade is the worst . . . and also
the best, as Jordan rides the ups and
downs of middle-school life in

THE BOY WHO FAILED DODGEBALL

1. Blood and Fireworks

In my almost-twelve years on this planet, I'd like to think I've learned a few things. So I've decided to share my hard-earned wisdom with all you other young people out there. Let's start with the best piece of advice I can possibly give you: Don't be born on a major national holiday. Sure, it's great that you will never have to go to school on your birthday. But being born on the Fourth of July nearly killed me.

Multiple times.

It started before I was even born. My dad, who is a psychiatrist, got drafted to be an army doctor in the Vietnam War just after my parents found out my mom was pregnant. By the time I came around, my mom, my dad, and my big sister, Lissa, lived on a big military base in Missouri called Fort Leonard Wood. My mom went into labor late at night on July 3, 1969, so my dad called the hospital. There were only two doctors on the staff who delivered babies, and one was off base for the big July 4 weekend. The other was at the base's massive holiday fireworks party, super drunk.

Anyway, my dad and a couple of the other base doctors

found the drunk guy, threw him in the shower, and gave him a whole lot of coffee. When my mom was ready to give birth, he was mostly just incredibly hungover. My mom saw that he looked kind of sick and shaky, so she made a deal with him. She said that if he delivered me safe and sound, she would name me after him.

His name was Ted. Not Theodore, just Ted.

I guess he didn't drop me or anything, because my parents named me Jordan Ted Sonnenblick.

Then there was the biggest July 4 ever: the Bicentennial. On July 4, 1976, when I turned seven, the country went all in on the grandest birthday celebration in its history. In Staten Island, New York, where I have lived since I was thirteen months old, kids painted every fire hydrant red, white, and blue. (The older kids let me paint two white stripes on the one at the end of my block!) New York Harbor, from the Statue of Liberty all the way to the Verrazano-Narrows Bridge, was packed with hundreds of tall sailing ships, big fancy yachts, fireboats, barges, and small speedboats. There were even dozens of US Navy ships. It was like a gigantic, very wet traffic jam.

A couple of days before the big event, teams of workers started to hang the largest American flag ever made between the two towers of the bridge. My richest friend, Steven Vitale, had a house on a big hill looking over the harbor, so my sister and I went over there to play with Steven and his sister and watch the flag go up. The girls were playing Hula-Hoop at the bottom of Steven's long, steep driveway while Steven and I took turns trying to skateboard down from the street to the house. This was kind of challenging, because the driveway wasn't perfectly smooth. It had lots of sharp pieces of gravel sticking up from the cement. Steven went inside for a drink break, but I decided to make one more run.

Somehow, just after I reached top speed, I lost my balance, went flying over the front of the board, and landed facedown.

My forehead must have hit one of those sharp pebbles. I think I was knocked out for a second, but it didn't hurt or anything. I stood up and started walking toward the girls, who took one look at me and ran screaming into the house. I couldn't figure out what was wrong until I felt something warm and wet dripping into my right eye.

Steven's mom came out, took me inside, and washed out the new dent in my forehead. By the time she was done bandaging me up, I was feeling pretty dizzy, so she took me to Steven's room, led me to the bed, and told me to rest. But Steven's room had a huge picture window that faced the water, and after a while, practice fireworks started going off.

If you've never gotten banged on the head, cut up, and knocked out, then locked in a room with the rockets' red glare and bombs bursting in air outside, I don't recommend it as a pleasure activity.

Two days later, I was feeling mostly recovered, aside from the intense itch that was coming from under the gauze pad just above my eyebrow. My whole family went to the roof of the building where my dad's office was. The building was only a block from the harbor, so we had the best view in town for the parade of ships and the fireworks display. Everybody got plates and filled them up with hamburgers and hot dogs. As we settled in to eat with all my dad's doctor friends and their kids, a question popped into my head that I just had to ask somebody.

For as long as I could remember, all the grown-ups in my family had told me that the July Fourth fireworks were for me. But there had never been a gazillion sailing ships, a two-hundred-foot-tall flag on a bridge, or a huge, official citywide fireworks display before. Had I done something special to deserve this? It was important to know, so I'd remember to do it again next year. I didn't know what *bicentennial* meant, and it was all pretty confusing. I turned to my dad's friend Dr. Accettola and asked, "Why is July Fourth such a big deal this year?"

"Because this year is the two hundredth," he replied.

"But I'm only seven!" I exclaimed.

That was when it hit me. The celebration wasn't in my honor at all. I took my plate behind a big brick chimney, sat with my back resting against the bricks, and cried.

All this time, I had thought I was famous. But really, I was just a little nobody.

Do yourself a favor. If you don't want a lifetime of danger

and heartbreak, be born on some random Tuesday in October. Or maybe March. March is nice.

Because here's the thing about being born on July 4. It teaches you to love fireworks. To wish for bigger and bigger fireworks. And to hope that one day, you'll be such a big deal that the big fireworks *are* for you.

2. Pick Your Heroes Carefully

I can't remember a time when I didn't love Evel Knievel, the greatest stuntman of all time. He isn't just the greatest stuntman. He's, like, the guy who invented the whole job of "stuntman." Before Evel Knievel, guys who crashed their motorcycles, broke multiple bones, and ended up in a coma were just considered unlucky. Evel Knievel turned the near-fatal motorcycle accident into an art form. By the time I was in kindergarten, practically every kid in my class wanted to be Evel Knievel. It looked like so much fun! He always wore a red-white-and-blue jumpsuit, and there were always thousands of cheering, screaming fans lined up to watch his stunts. Wherever Evel went, the fireworks really *were* for him.

I remember being at my Aunt Iris's house in New Jersey when I was five, gathered around with all my cousins to wait for Evel Knievel's famous rocket jump across Snake River Canyon in Idaho. It was so incredible! The jump distance was more than a quarter of a mile! I didn't know what a quarter of a mile was, but it sounded like a lot. Evel got lowered into his custom Skycycle rocket by crane, two assistants strapped him into his seat and put his helmet on, and then we all held our breath.

The Skycycle shot up the gigantic ramp at 350 miles an hour. We cheered as it flew upward into the air over the canyon. Then the disaster happened: The parachute that was supposed to slow the Skycycle down at the end opened too early. We all sat there in shock as the TV announcers said Evel and his Skycycle were going to land in the rushing rapids of the canyon!

It was almost a bummer when he survived with only a broken nose.

That was the thing about Evel Knievel. You could never tell which was cooler: his successes or his failures. I mean, in his very first major stunt, before I was even born, he was trying to jump a motorcycle over a ninety-foot-long box of rattlesnakes and land between two mountain lions. Making the jump would have been amazing enough. But he actually landed a bit short and broke through the far end of the box, freeing the rattlesnakes as the crowd fled in horror.

Angry rattlesnakes everywhere?

Legendary.

It might seem nutty to idolize a guy who holds the Guinness record for the most broken bones in a lifetime. But kids in my class show up every year with Evel Knievel lunch boxes. I don't think I have ever met a boy who didn't have at least one or two Evel Knievel action figures lying around his room. The smart kids leave it right there. The maniacs like me have

spent their entire childhoods trying to live up to the legend.

On my block, we are all in on the stuntman lifestyle. We spend hours putting together ramps. We have short ramps. We have long ramps. We have steep ramps and gradual ramps. We even have ramps that make you land on other ramps.

Don't try that one at home.

Have there been injuries? You *bet* there have been injuries! Riding on my original bicentennial-model

Schwinn bike that looked like an Evel Knievel tribute with its stars-and-stripes paint job, my friend Peter Friedman once flew over the handlebars right in front of my house and left a skid mark made of skin on the street. Dougie Kaner, who lived two doors down from me until he moved to a new house last year, once landed on his chin and needed to get stitches. Then there was the time I was timing myself racing down the street and flew over the handlebars, removing all the skin from my left shoulder. My mom, who saw the whole thing from our front window, was afraid to come out of the house and roll me over, because she was literally afraid my whole face would be gone.

For a while, our favorite bike game was chicken, which involves two guys riding their bikes at each other at top speed to see who swerves first. That lasted until the Great Head-On Collision of 1978, in which Dougie and I *both* flew over the handlebars and knocked heads in midair.

If flying over the handlebars becomes an Olympic sport, the training center will be my block.

Then there was last year's most popular pastime, Kill the Guy on the Green Machine. I am sure you've all seen a Green Machine. You know, the grass-colored plastic tricycle with the small back wheels, the gigantic front wheel, and the two levers you yank if you want to steer? Well, for a while on our block, we would borrow a Green Machine from Eric Warheit, the younger kid who lived between my house and Dougie's, and then the brutal spectacle would begin as five or six other guys tried to deliberately crash into it.

What I figured out before anybody else is that the guy on the Green Machine is actually safer than the guys on the bikes chasing him, because his back is protected by a hard plastic seat and his front is protected by the gigantic wheel. Honestly, the only way the Green Machine rider can lose is if one of the bicycle riders attacks from the side and somehow manages to get his bike's front wheel between the edge of the Green Machine's seat and the mounting for the steering levers. That's only maybe a foot of room. Much more often, anybody who crashes into the Green Machine flies over his bike's handlebars.

At one point, the flying-over-the-handlebars thing got so out of hand that Dougie's mom said, "You know, somebody should really invent some kind of a . . . I don't know . . . a helmet for kids to wear when they ride bikes." Dougie and I laughed about that one for days.

I crash into things on purpose so often that you might even think I am fearless. But I have a secret nobody knows:

I am secretly terrified almost all the time.

I am scared I will die from an asthma attack.

I am scared that my three remaining grandparents will get cancer and die like my Nana Adele did when I was in second grade.

Most of all, for years and years, I have spent every Monday and Wednesday night lying awake in bed, afraid that my mom will crash her car on the forty-minute drive home from her night classes at Rutgers University in New Jersey.

Some people might think I am weird because I spend so much of my time and energy inventing new ways of crashing into stuff when I'm so scared of everything. But that isn't the really weird part. The really weird part is that the only time I am not afraid of death is when I am doing things that are actually death-defying.

Being in danger is one of the only things that makes me feel safe.

3. SEPTEMBER

If you think about it, sixth grade is a really terrible idea. You spend your whole life watching the big kids head off to middle school, and you think they seem so cool and grown-up. They're laughing with their friends, bragging about trouble they've gotten into and out of, teasing each other about crushes—which all makes middle school sound a million times more exciting than elementary school. By the end of fifth grade, you can't *wait* for the fall, and your daring new life of adventure.

Then September actually arrives, and you realize that sixth grade is a terrifying downhill death ride on hostile, shifting terrain. All of a sudden, you are with kids from like four different elementary schools. Everybody who was the best at something in the spring is just another nobody now. Were you the fastest kid at P.S. 45? News flash: You might not even be in the top ten at I.S. 61. Did you think that being the smartest kid at P.S. 16 made you special? Just wait till you see what the kids from P.S. 31 know already. There's a junior chess master from 45, a girl from 16 who has been in three

TV commercials already, a concert piano champion from 31.

And that's just the sixth grade. The seventh and eighth graders are even more advanced. Talented. *Huge*.

But your classmates are only one of the challenges you face. Instead of having to figure out one teacher who's going to be with you the whole day, you have a gajillion different teachers, and they all have different personalities. Some might be friendly. Some might be mean. Some might be the type that starts out seeming mean but is really friendly once you get to know them. And it's a sure thing that some are going to seem nice at first but *turn out* to be mean.

And every teacher wants you to have different supplies. Each one has a different way of assigning seats. Some want you to raise your hand and ask before you cross the room to sharpen your pencil. Some bark, "Why are you wasting my time asking whether you can walk fifteen feet? Do I look like your *mom*?"

But if you snap back, "No, my mom is pretty," *you're* the one who gets in trouble.

Then there are the rules of the school: the official ones that tell you things like when you can go to your locker and what kind of dorky gym shorts you have to buy, and the real, semi-secret ones like, "Never, ever use the bathroom outside the gym on the Concourse. Ever. EVER."

I haven't even mentioned the incredibly dense crowds in the hallways, the swarming hive of the cafeteria, the utter chaos of dismissal, or the nonstop noise. The night before my first day at I.S. 61, it all hits me. For months, I thought I was ready for this, but I'm not.

I am picturing the beginning of middle school as an extremely rapid, terrifying, and uncontrolled ride straight into a wall.

As it turns out, I am not so far off.